Nature in German History

NATURE IN GERMAN HISTORY

Edited by
Christof Mauch

Berghahn Books
New York • Oxford

Published in 2004 by

Berghahn Books

© 2004 Christof Mauch

Library of Congress Cataloging-in-Publication Data

Nature in German history / edited by Christof Mauch.
  p. cm.
  ISBN 1-57181-438-8
  1. Human ecology--Germany--History. 2. Philosophy of nature--Germany--History. 3.
Human beings--Effect of enviornment on--Germany--History. 4. Geographical
perception--Germany--Philosophy. 5. Germany--Environmental conditions. I. Mauch,
Christof.

GFS576.N37 2004
304.2'0943--dc22   2004045134

British Library Cataloguing in Publication Data

A catalogue record for this book is available
from the British Library.

Printed in the United States on acid-free paper.

CONTENTS

CONTRIBUTORS

David Blackbourn, Coolidge Professor of Modern History, Harvard University.

Franz-Josef Brüggemeier, Professor of Social, Economic and Environmental History, University of Freiburg

Sandra Chaney, Associate Professor of History, Erskine College

Marc Cioc, Professor of History, University of California at Santa Cruz

Christof Mauch, Director of the German Historical Institute, Washington, DC, and Professor of Modern History, University of Cologne.

Linda Parshall, Professor Emerita of German Studies, Portland State University

Joachim Wolschke-Bulmahn, Professor of Open Space Planning and Garden Culture, University of Hannover

PREFACE

This collection has its origins in a lecture series that took place at the German Historical Institute, Washington, DC, in the fall of 1999. In preparing the series, the organizers and speakers came to the realization that there was no overview of the subject of nature in German history available in English. Toward filling this gap, the speakers graciously agreed to revise their lectures for publication. All involved in this project realize that this collection does not offer a comprehensive survey of the subject. Despite the broad chronological, geographic, and thematic range of the essays presented here, there are indisputable gaps. Nonetheless, this collection does give a sampling of the diverse approaches scholars are taking in addressing the key issues in the environmental history of Germany. Taken together, these essays illustrate the ways that environmental questions have come to figure prominently in German cultural, political, and economic life.

I want to thank all the contributors for agreeing to add to their already formidable workloads by agreeing first to speak at the German Historical Institute and then to revise for publication. Several of the contributors presented work in progress during the lecture series, so preparing an essay for this collection meant taking on considerable additional work. I want also to thank David Lazar of the German Historical Institute for his help in preparing the manuscript for submission. Our publisher, Dr. Marion Berghahn, deserves a word of thanks for her support of this project and her considerable patience.

Christof Mauch

INTRODUCTION
Nature and Nation in Transatlantic Perspective

Christof Mauch

I

Writing about Robert Frost, the poet Joseph Brodsky contrasted European and American sensibilities. "When a European ... encounters a tree, it's a tree made familiar by history, to which it's been a witness. This or that king sat underneath it, laying down this or that law," Brodsky writes. "Whereas when an American walks out of his house and encounters a tree it is a meeting of equals. Man and tree face each other in their respective primal power, free of references: neither has a past, and as to whose future is greater, it is a toss-up. Basically, it's epidermis meeting bark."[1]

Nature itself transcends national borders, but landscapes have often taken on nationalistic meanings. From the time the colonies declared their independence, some Americans have understood that the country's unique landscapes could serve as a foundation for national identity and also as basis for comparison and subtle competition with Europe.[2] In his *Notes on the State of Virginia*, for example, Thomas Jefferson described the Potomac gorge near Harper's Ferry as a "scene ... worth a voyage across the Atlantic."[3] Topography, climate, vegetation, water and its absence, all have figured prominently in historians' narratives of the settling of the North American continent. Americans, unlike Europeans, saw themselves at war with nature well into the nineteenth century. The emergence of an American culture out of the wilderness is the grand narrative of U.S. historiography. Frederick Jackson Turner, one of America's most influential historians, went so far as to argue that even American democracy has its origins in the human encounter with trees, "in the forest."[4]

Americans have analyzed their relationship with nature much more thoroughly than other peoples. Apart from the obvious historical importance of natural catastrophes—the 1906 San Francisco earthquake and the Dust Bowl of the 1930s, for instance[5]—probably the most important reason behind this engagement is the late "discovery" and settlement of the North American continent. At the time when Britain, France, and Germany were becoming increasingly urban and industrialized, hundreds of thousands of settlers, many of them recent immigrants from Europe, were establishing farms, ranches, and towns throughout the regions that eventually became the continental United States. They struggled with wetlands and arid zones, and their stories became part of an enduring myth that linked nature and history.[6]

Migration and settlement of similar scope and impact occurred in Central Europe, too. But even though these encounters with the environment occurred in the distant past, the notion of pristine, untainted nature played a part in German ideas of national identity well into the postwar era, as Sandra Chaney explains in her contribution to this volume.[7] Indeed, the word *Heimat*, the evocative term for homeland or hometown, was virtually synonymous with "nature" through much of German history.[8]

The ways in which nature and national identity are connected are often more obvious to foreign observers than to natives. Alexandre Dumas, for instance, informed his fellow Frenchmen that the Rhine was profoundly venerated by the Germans. For the Germans, he explained, "the Rhine is might, ... it has passions like a man or like a God."[9] Alexis de Tocqueville, on the other hand, pointed out in his *Democracy in America*: "In Europe people talk a great deal of the wilds of America, but the Americans themselves never think about them."[10]

Ideas about nature, in short, are often closely bound up with notions of national identity: thus, the nation, although an entirely human construct, is indeed a viable unit for considering the history of the environment. And since natives and foreigners do not necessarily see the connections between perceptions of nature and of national identity in the same way, it certainly makes sense to take account of the views of both. This collection, accordingly, brings together studies by German and American scholars.

II

Perhaps the most enduring myth in the history of nature and the German mind is the special relationship that Germans have developed with trees and woods over the centuries. No landscape has been identified more closely with German history than *der deutsche Wald*, the German forest. When the Germans established a conservation society in 1947 for the sole purpose of protecting trees, the very name of this organization—*Schutzgemeinschaft Deutscher Wald* (SDW, Society for the Protection of the German Forest)—suggested that there was *one unitary* German forest. In reality, the German landscape was made up of a diverse set of regional parks and woods.[11] It is no coincidence, then, that trees feature prominently in several of the contributions to this volume.

Tacitus noted the German tribes' attachment to their *silvis horrida,* their horrid forest, in his *De Germania.* The world north of the Alps appeared wild and threatening to this Roman writer, who was used to walled cities (*urbes*) and open Mediterranean landscapes, not to swamps and forests.[12] Tacitus was not impressed with the Teutonic woods and their sylvan charms. But when the Germans in the age of Enlightenment began to write their first scientific forest histories, they always quoted *De Germania* as evidence that great extended forests had once covered their country. There can be little doubt that Tacitus had an impact on the afforestation efforts of the eighteenth century that were meant to restore the *alterthümlicher Zustand der Natur,* the putative "ancient condition of nature."

In his famous speech on "Man and the Earth," German philosopher Ludwig Klages deplored the loss of nature in the age of industrialization. The "ancient trees," he complained, were being replaced by "forests of chimneys" everywhere.[13] Klages's audience had gathered to commemorate the German victory against Napoleon in 1813. His appeal thus suggested that resistance *pro patria* was linked to the duty of protecting nature in general and restoring the German forest in particular. Klage and his contemporaries believed that some woods in Germany dating from the eighteenth century were thousands of years old. Conservationist Konrad Günther, for instance, claimed that forests pristine in appearance, such as the *Hasbrucher Wald,* were a "monument from old Germanic times" that "tell us more about the life of our forbears than ramparts and walls."[14]

For over a century now, tens of thousands of Germans have been making pilgrimages, typically on a Sunday afternoon, to the oldest trees of their regions, visiting their timbered friends, such as the *Hölzlekönig* and *Hölzlekönigin* (the King and Queen of the Woods) in the *Baar* highland in southwest Germany. Local newspapers routinely report on the history and the decay of these trees. Some venerable trees have actually been equipped with lightning rods to protect them from damage—by nature!—and preserve their legacy.

In his *Geschichte des Waldes,* ecologist Hansjörg Küster mentions a conversation between his grandfather and a British reeducation officer right after the Second World War. The conversation was pleasant until his grandfather mentioned Grimm's fairy tales. "Oh no," the British officer waved him off, "oh no, that's too much forest."[15] Whereas German nationalists and Romantics held to the myth that the real Germany had been lost with the disappearance of the German *Urwald,* non-Germans like Tacitus and the British reeducation officer were inclined to identify the "horrid" forest with barbarism.

Given the emotionally charged relationship between Germans and their trees, one can understand that Berlin mayor Ernst Reuter called the destruction of the city's wooded central park, the Tiergarten, during World War II "the most painful wound that Berlin had suffered from the war."[16]

By the same token, it is hardly surprising that the Germans were the first to lament the loss of the forests when it became known that acid rain from sulfur dioxide and nitrogen oxide emissions did tremendous damage to coniferous trees, particularly in industrial countries.[17] The term *Waldsterben*—"forest death"—

became a mantra for Green environmentalism that quickly entered the vocabulary of several languages and triggered numerous projects to improve air quality, address urban pollution, and protect the natural environment. A lively debate took place in Germany toward the end of the twentieth century over the nature and extent of damage to the forests. In his contribution to this volume, Franz-Josef Brüggemeier uses the debate on *Waldsterben* to consider the methodological difficulties that both scientists and historians face in trying to give a true estimate of the damage and, more generally, the changes that have occurred in the natural environment over time.

German historians have been more interested in urban environmental issues over the past thirty years than their American counterparts, who have focused on wilderness, agriculture, and parks. They have discussed pollution and waste, and the costs of industrialization. Their methodological approaches have been predominantly socio-economic,[18] and the questions they have asked are often informed by present-day environmental issues such as the risks of nuclear power. The dramatic rise in the 1980s of the *Grüne*, the Green Party, contributed not only to a high degree of environmental consciousness in German society as a whole but also to more critical approaches in environmental research.

Another factor underlying the cultural differences between German and American approaches to environmental history is the lack of large "unspoilt" areas in Germany. American environmental historians have written extensively about America's national monuments, the national parks, and tourism.[19] Most studies in U.S. environmental history assume that nature is quintessentially American and that the United States is indeed "Nature's Nation."[20] The connection between landscape and patriotic identity has contributed to the popularity of research on "American spaces"[21] and to the visibility of environmental history in the United States. One U.S. scholar has even suggested that historians should "shamelessly … revive patriotism" in America in order to further the success of the preservation movement.[22] Such advice would certainly not be well received in Germany, where memories of the Nazi period—when the German landscape became an emblem of totalitarianism, as Joachim Wolschke-Bulmahn explains in his contribution to this volume—are very strong.[23]

Nature is never neutral. We see it through the lens of our ideas and ideals. In Germany, the political overtones are especially distinct. The story of the protection of the natural environment in Germany can never be told as a success story as it is in the U.S. The extermination of native plants in Eastern Europe by Nazi conservationists who wished to "germanize" the landscape was carried out simultaneously with the extermination of millions of lives.[24] The term "German space" therefore has sinister connotations. References to nature as victim or to "lost" spaces evoke very different associations and memories in Germany than in other countries. Critical environmental consciousness and patriotism are not linked in present-day Germany.

III

All the essays in this volume are informed by three fundamental insights: first, that nature is in constant change; second, that our ideas of nature change over time; and third, that these ideas shape our relationship with nature and thereby the natural environment itself.

As much as we tend to hold a fixed image of nature—in our collective memories, in landscape paintings, or in preservation efforts—we have to keep in mind that *nature changes*, season by season and year by year. Until the 1940s, the predominant view among scientists was that nature, if left alone, would ultimately reach a condition of stability and balance, a so-called natural climax. German conservationists in the 1930s, among them forester Arnold Freiherr von Vietinghoff-Riesch, believed that nature would reach a "state of perfection" (*Vollendungszustand, Klimax)* and should be left alone once it had reached this state. [25] When, as a result of their ideology, the Nazis ignored the concept of sustainability, the consequences were disastrous. Some woods were left to themselves in order to provide a natural backdrop for the "ideal state"; other areas were entirely deforested—in order to serve the war effort. It was not until the 1950s that the holistic view—a belief-system accepted on both sides of the Atlantic—was shaken and that scientists recognized how unstable ecosystems really are, how dynamic and wild and unpredictable nature is.[26] *Waldsterben*, whatever the cause may be, reminds us of the changes that come with the cycle of life.

The great time span covered by the essays in this volume illustrates the second fundamental insight: that our minds play a major role in uncovering the *meaning of nature* and that the meanings we assign *change over time*. During the medieval and early modern periods, nature was perceived as wild and dangerous. In Germany, this view prepared the ground for efforts to shape or tame the natural environment during the Enlightenment. Once tamed, nature was no longer threatening. It could be controlled and put to use. In their essays, respectively, on the Prussian marshlands and the Rhine, David Blackbourn and Marc Cioc provide examples of this shift in thinking about nature.

The German Romantics introduced yet another phase in the evolution of attitudes toward the physical environment. From their perspective, the benefits of nature were not to be found in cultivation or exploitation of natural resources but in the beauty of nature, in its non-material and spiritual values. For philosophers of the Romantic period, landscapes had the potential to elicit a sense of the sublime. Informed by Rousseau's insight that "existence was a succession of moments perceived through the senses," the Romantics rallied against the Enlightenment (or absolutist) view that natural phenomena are governed by classical logic and objective rules.[27] The meaning of nature stemmed, rather, from subjective perception or intuition. Romantic philosophers and landscape architects put forward aesthetic theories and landscape plans that replaced formality with a new naturalism. Nature was glorified because of the emotional sensations it created. In her contribution to this volume, Linda Parshall examines the ideas and career of one of the most famous German landscape architects, Prince Hermann Pückler-Muskau, the "green prince of Germany" whose gardens were constructed to idealize nature and transform reality into a poetic picture of an unspoilt past. [28] Pückler-Muskau's garden was an island in an increasingly urbanized and industrialized world. The meaning he and his contemporaries attributed to nature remained restricted to a small elite. [29] The essay by Joachim Wolschke-Bulmahn on the transformation of ideas about wilderness in German landscape architecture provides a larger framework for the Muskau case study.

The concept of the pristine character and "uncivilized" forms of nature that developed in the course of the nineteenth century were important factors for a wider appreciation of nature, particularly by the middle classes. The *Heimatbewegung* (homeland movement) became the most important driving force for a new understanding of the environment. [30] Nature was now seen as a noble space of leisure and recreation and as a refuge from the "nervous sphere" of industry and urbanity. [31] The defense of *Heimat* and the defense of nature became almost synonymous, at least in the realm of rhetoric. This was to change only in the 1970s, as Sandra Chaney shows in her essay here on nature and ideology in postwar West Germany, as new ideas about the environment underscoring the importance of healthy, unpolluted nature to human health and well-being gained currency. The appreciation of a healthy *Umwelt* (environment) became of more immediate importance, especially to city-dwellers, than the idea of an untainted *Heimat.* At the same time, concerns about pollution, widely promoted by the media, took center stage, as Franz-Josef Brüggemeier points out in his essay on *Waldsterben.*

Taken together, the essays presented here leave no doubt that the meanings attached to nature have changed over time: from nature as something to be feared to nature as something to be appreciated; from a specific philosophical concept to a collective belief system; from a concept identified with cultural space to one identified with health. These different meanings did not emerge one after the other in neat chronological order, but the shifts in thinking about nature can nonetheless be incorporated within the larger framework of German political and cultural history.

The third insight the essays of this volume provide—that our ideas shape our relationship with nature and thereby the natural environment itself—is perhaps the most important one. While nature itself and the meanings we identify with it are in constant change, our minds also play a crucial role in our interaction with the physical environment—in our decisions to try to tame or manipulate nature, for instance, or to preserve complex natural habitats. David Blackbourn's essay in this collection outlines the ambitions of an absolute ruler who set out to drain seemingly "barbarous" marshlands and the means he employed to do so. Marc Cioc demonstrates how utilitarian ideals turned an untamed and meandering Rhine into a functional, fast-flowing channel. Linda Parshall discusses the ways in which one German princeling manipulated nature in order to create a vast landscape park consistent with his vision of an aesthetic and social utopia.

Joachim Wolschke-Bulmahn explains how Germans over the centuries designed gardens and landscapes as symbolic arenas for imagined and political worlds. Sandra Chaney shows how the transformation of environmental consciousness in postwar Germany translated into the creation of urban and state parks all across the country, and Franz-Josef Brüggemeier discusses the relationship between public concern for nature and science.

All these essays suggest that nature has a place both in physical reality and in our minds. They see nature as more than something "out there" but also as something more than a social or cultural construction. Taken together, the essays demonstrate that our images of nature can be translated into social and economic, architectural and scientific, political and environmental activity.

Historians of the environment have often been accused of being politically motivated.[32] This is in fact hardly ever the case, certainly not in the essays presented here. Nevertheless, the insights that this volume conveys are indeed political. They demonstrate that the relationship between humanity and nature is one of "multiple feedback effects" and that there is much more room for maneuver in (re)shaping this relationship than one might at first assume.[33] The story of nature in Germany is not one of loss, but of change. A historical approach to nature presents us with the opportunity to study the evolution of ideas and activities as they relate to nature. Many ideas are specific to the German experience, but most are also paradigmatic and relevant for the study of nature everywhere. They provide us with insights into the role of technology in managing and changing nature, into the influence of extreme (totalitarian) ideology on ideas of nature, and into nature and environmental consciousness in an increasingly urban world with ever fewer, ever smaller patches of wilderness.

Notes

1. Joseph Brodsky, "Grief and Reason," in: Joseph Brodsky, Seamus Heaney, and Derek Walcott, *Homage to Robert Frost* (New York, 1996), 7-8.
2. On the early debates between Abbé de Pauw, Comte de Buffon, and Guillaume-Thomas, Abbé de Raynal, see John Opie, *Nature's Nation: An Environmental History of the United States* (Forth Worth, 1998), 51-54. In Europe, nature in general and the topography of landscapes in particular were closely connected to specific regional or national (but not European) identities: see Simon Schama, *Landscape and Memory* (New York, 1995).
3. Thomas Jefferson, *Notes on the State of Virginia*. Edited with an introduction and noted by Frank Shuffelton (New York, 1999), 20.
4. Frederick Jackson Turner, *The Frontier in American History*. Foreword by Wilbur R. Jacobs (Tuscon, 1986).
5. See, e.g., Donald Worster, *Dust Bowl: The Southern Plains in the 1930s* (New York, 1979); Mike Davis, *Ecology of Fear: Los Angeles and the Imagination of Disaster* (New York, 1998).

6. Ann Vileisis, *Discovering the Unknown Landscape: A History of America's Wetlands* (Washington, D.C./ Covelo, CA., 1999); Richard White, *"It's Your Misfortune and None of My Own": A New History of the American West* (Norman, OK, 1993); William Beinart and Peter Coates, *Environment and History: The Taming of Nature in the USA and South Africa* (London, 1995).

7. See also Rudy Koshar, *Germany's Transient Pasts: Preservation and National Memory in the Twentieth Century* (Chapel Hill, 1998).

8. Celia Applegate, *A Nation of Provincials: The German Idea of Heimat* (Berkeley, 1990).

9. "Il est difficile, à nous autres Francais, de comprendre quelle véneration profonde les Allemands ont pour le Rhin ... le Rhin c'est la force; le Rhin c'est l' independance; le Rhin c'est la liberté. La Rhin a des passions comme un homme ou plutot comme un Dieu." Alexandre Dumas, *Excursions sur les bords du Rhin.* With an introduction and vocabulary by Théodore Henckels (New York, 1905), 11.

10. Alexis de Tocqueville, *Democracy in America*, ed. Phillips Bradley. 2 vols. (New York, 1945) 2: 74.

11. Raymond H. Dominick III, *The Environmental Movement in Germany: Prophets and Pioneers, 1871-1971* (Bloomington, 1992), 134-135. See also Sandra Chaney's essay in this volume and Wilhelm Lienenkämpfer, *Grüne Welt zu treuen Händen: Naturschutz und Landschaftspflege im Industriezeitalter* (Stuttgart, 1963).

12. "Terra, etsi aliquanto specie differet, in universum aut silvis horrida aut paludibus foeda." Publius Cornelius Tacitus, *The Germania and Agricola With Notes for Colleges by W.S. Tyler* (New York and London, 1847), 15-41, 18.

13. Ludwig Klages, *Mensch und Erde: Sieben Abhandlungen*, third ed. (Jena, 1929), 9-41, 23.

14. Konrad Guenther, *Der Naturschutz* (Freiburg i.Br., 1910), quoted in Hansjörg Küster, *Geschichte des Waldes: Von der Urzeit bis zur Gegenwart* (Munich, 1998), 209. See also Kurt Borchers, *Der Wald als deutsches Volksgut* (Lüneburg, 1948).

15. Küster, *Geschichte des Waldes*, 8.

16. When the British donated trees and plants in 1952 and opened what was called an *Englischer Garten* in the heart of the *Tiergarten*, this project was interpreted by contemporaries as part of a larger process of coming to terms with the past. Folkwin Wendland, "Die historische Entwicklung des Großen Tiergartens in Berlin," in Landesdenkmalamt Berlin, ed., *Der Berliner Tiergarten: Vergangenheit und Zukunft* (Berlin, 1996), 7-33; Katrin Lesser-Sayrac, "Willy Alverdes—sein Werk als Gartenarchitekt und seine Verdienste für den Großen Tiergarten in Berlin," in: ibid., 34-62.

17. Karl Friedrich Wentzel, "Hat der Wald noch eine Zukunft?" in Bernd Weyergraf, ed., *Waldungen: Die Deutschen und ihr Wald* (Berlin: Akademie der Künste, 1987), 102-112.

18. See the research reports by Joachim Radkau, "Technik- und Umweltgeschichte," *Geschichte in Wissenschaft und Unterricht* 48 (1997): 479-496; 50 (1999): 250-258, 356-384, and the bibliography in Franz-Josef Brüggemeier, *Tschernobyl, 26. April 1986: Die ökologische Herausforderung* (Munich, 1998), 297-300.

19. Cp. Hal Rothman, *America's National Monuments: The Politics of Preservation* (Lawrence, KS, 1989); Richard West Sellars, *Preserving Nature in the National Parks: A History* (New Haven, 1997); David M. Wrobel and Patrick T. Long, eds. *Seeing and Being Seen: Tourism in the American West* (Lawrence, KS, 2001); Paul Sutter, *Driven Wild: How the Fight Against Automobiles Launched the Modern Wilderness Movement* (Seattle, 2002).

20. In April 2000, for example, the European Association for American Studies dedicated its biennial conference in Graz, Austria, to the topic "Nature's Nation Reconsidered: American Concepts of Nature from Wonder to Ecological Crisis."

21. The term "American Space" has been used many times since John Brinckerhoff Jackson introduced it in his groundbreaking monograph, *American Space: The Centennial Years, 1865-1876* (New York, 1972).

22. U.S. historian of the American West Patricia Limerick points out that national pride was an important factor in the early years of the preservation movement's success. She therefore sug-

gests that one should "revive patriotism, and appeal to it often and shamelessly." Patricia Nelson Limerick, *Something in the Soil: Legacies and Reckonings in the New West* (New York, 2000), 182.

23. Interestingly, the Nazis labeled the ruthless technological exploitation of nature as "Americanization" while at the same time they identified "untouched nature" with "Germanness." This line of thought is most clearly spelled out in a book by Alwin Seifert, *Im Zeitalter des Lebendigen: Natur, Heimat, Technik* (Dresden and Planegg, 1941). See also Gert Grönig and Joachim Wolschke-Bulmahn, *Die Liebe zur Landschaft Teil III: Der Drang nach Osten. Zur Entwicklung der Landespflege im Nationalsozialismus und während des Zweiten Weltkrieges in den 'eingegliederten Ostgebieten'* (Munich, 1997).

24. Wendy Lower, "A New Ordering of Space and Race: Nazi Colonial Dreams in Zhytomyr, Ukraine, 1941-1944," *German Studies Review* 25 (2002): 227-254; Jürgen Zimmerer, "Colonialism and the Holocaust: Towards an Archaelogy of Genocide" in: A. Dirk Moses, ed., *Genocide and Settler Society: Frontier Violence and the "Civilizing Process" in Australia* (forthcoming).

25. Arnold, Forstmeister Frhr von Vietinghoff-Riesch, *Naturschutz: Eine nationalpolitische Kulturaufgabe* (Neudamm und Berlin, 1936).

26. On the debate between the holistic view and the reductionist theory of the 1950s, see Michael G. Barbour, "Ecological Fragmentation in the Fifties," in: William Cronon, ed., *Uncommon Ground: Toward Reunifying Nature* (New York, 1995), 233-255.

27. Philip Pregill and Nancy Volkman, *Landscapes in History: Design and Planning in the Eastern and Western Traditions,* second ed. (New York, 1999), 244.

28. Adrian von Buttlar, "Gartentheorie um die Wende zum 19. Jahrhundert," in *Peter Joseph Lenné: Volkspark und Arkadien,* Florian von Buttlar, ed. (Berlin, 1989), 25-30; Adrian von Buttlar, *Der Landschaftsgarten: Gartenkunst des Klassizismus und der Romantik* (Cologne, 1989); Gottfried Zirnstein, *Ökologie und Umwelt in der Geschichte* (Marburg 1996), 98-103; Pregill and Volkman, *Landscapes in History,* 233-263.

29. Frederick Law Olmsted spoke for many American landscape architects when he criticized private parks as "a monopoly, in a very peculiar manner, of a very few, very rich people." Frederick Law Olmsted, *Yosemite and the Mariposa Grove: A Preliminary Report 1865.* Introduction by Victoria Post Ranney (Yosemite, CA, 1993), 17-18.

30. Karl Ditt, "Die deutsche Heimatbewegung 1871-1945," in Will Cremer and Ansgar Klein, eds. *Heimat.* Vol. 1, *Analysen, Themen, Perspektiven* (Bielefeld, 1990), 135-154; Edeltraut Klueting, ed., *Antimodernismus und Reform: Beiträge zur Geschichte der deutschen Heimatbewegung* (Darmstadt, 1991).

31. William H. Rollins, *A Greener Vision of Home: Cultural Politics and Environmental Reform in the German Heimatschutz Movement* (Ann Arbor, 1997); Klaus Bergmann, *Agrarromantik und Großstadtfeindschaft* (Meisenheim am Glan, 1970); Joachim Radkau, *Das Zeitalter der Nervosität: Deutschland zwischen Bismarck und Hitler* (Munich, 1998).

32. Andrew Rowell, *Green Backlash: Global Subversion of the Environmental Movement* (London and New York, 1996).

33. Helmut Jäger, *Einführung in die Umweltgeschichte* (Darmstadt, 1994), 11.

Chapter 1

"CONQUESTS FROM BARBARISM"
Taming Nature in Frederick the Great's Prussia

David Blackbourn

Many people have commented on the recent popular success enjoyed by memoir writers, but another trend has passed largely unnoticed. I refer to the appearance on the bestseller list of books that depict human frailty in the face of mighty natural forces. Examples include Jon Krakauer's *Into Thin Air*, about a disastrous attempt on Everest, and Sebastian Junger's *A Perfect Storm*, on the fatal effects of a 1991 Nor'easter. It is not only recent events that have been treated in this way. Erik Larson has enjoyed huge success with a book on the storm that devastated the American Gulf Coast in 1900, writing of "the fury and folly around the turn-of-the-century hurricane that destroyed Galveston."[1] His melodramatic words neatly summarize two key elements of the genre: the fury of nature, the folly of humans' belief in their own invincibility. A similar intellectual impulse animates several new or reissued books about human encounters with the Arctic and Antarctic, works that catalogue how the power of the ice mocked human aspirations. One of the most thoughtful comes from the Austrian writer Christoph Ransmayr, *The Terror of the Ice and the Darkness*, an artful blend of history and fiction based on an Austro-Hungarian North Pole expedition of the 1870s.[2]

We could call this genre "Nature Fights Back." Books like these are no doubt partly a result of larger trends in the media world. At a time when U.S. cable outlets like the Weather Channel and Discovery have proved that it pays to dramatize extreme events, even the elements are subject to the cult of celebrity. The naming of tropical storms and hurricanes means that Andrew and Floyd slip effortlessly into our lives alongside Monica and Elian. But these works are also attuned to our environmentally troubled cast of mind. Tapping into a modern

Notes for this section begin on page 26.

concern with disappearing wetlands, desertification and global warming, they point to the limits of human mastery over the natural world. As such they restate an older idea that Nature with an upper-case "N" is awesome and sublime. It is not, or should not be, just there for the taking.

Most of the people in the essay that follows believed that Nature *was* there for the taking. It was powerful, yes, even hostile and vengeful; but it could be mastered. Let me offer you some verse written in 1848, year of European revolutions. It describes "a mighty vassal" in the Prussian marches, who "stormed through hearth and home" until a royal hero "drove him from the field." The following stanzas provide the answer:

> The vanquished power is our River Oder
> And its terrain the Oder Marshes
> The hero who cast him in chains
> Has risen to the vault of heaven

> Now the enemy is agitating once again
> And threatens war anew
> But as the noble spirit has not disappeared
> From Old Fritz's throne
> Renewed victory beckons[3]

This undistinguished verse introduces my central theme: human mastery over the natural world. The author was a Prussian dike inspector, Carl Heuer, and he was referring to the draining and settlement of the Oderbruch one hundred years earlier, one of the best known of many such projects during the reign of Frederick the Great. These undertakings are the subject of the essay: the motives that drove them, how they were realized, the resistance they encountered, and their double-edged effects.

I am interested, on the one hand, in the material, physical process of transformation, for it seems to me that the time is ripe for the historical pendulum to swing back some way towards the material. Not all places are "imagined."[4] But the essay will also be concerned with what people thought they were doing and in what those who opposed them thought *they* were doing, too. As Carl Heuer's doggerel suggests, undertakings like draining the Oder marshes were heavy with political and cultural meanings. How could it be otherwise? Even more than the other elements, water has lent itself to a wide variety of metaphorical uses, from creation myths onwards. A German historian thinks of Leopold von Ranke's idea that History, like a river, "flowed," or of the ways that nineteenth-century conservatives represented revolution as a "flood" against which "dikes" had to be erected. Conversely, it makes sense to attend to the language in which contemporaries wrote about hydrological enterprises, for it would be a mistake to view them in narrowly technical terms. Neither the history of technology nor environmental history can usefully be separated from political history or the history of mentalities. In that respect, the ambition of the original *Annales* school of historians remains exemplary. Total history is impossible, but (like objectivity) we can aspire to it.

This essay is principally concerned with what happened to Prussian marsh and fen in the eighteenth century. I am not suggesting that nothing of relevance happened before then or implying any simple distinction between "pre-modern" and "modern" eras. One virtue of environmental history is its long sweep, its capacity to call into question narratives that turn on a premodern/modern axis, especially narratives closely linked to industrialization. Attempts to tame and harness German waters were, of course, legion in the medieval period, whether undertaken by the Teutonic Knights, the Cistercians, or others. The sixteenth and seventeenth centuries then witnessed mounting activity to drain and settle land in areas such as East Friesland, the Jeverland, and Schleswig-Holstein, in addition to the "Dutch" colonies or *Holländereien* established in Prussia by Frederick William the Great Elector.[5] It would be quite misleading to see the areas of marshland tackled by Frederick the Great as existing in some kind of pristine "natural" state.

Figure 1. The Lower Oderbruch before the great drainage project of 1747-53: detail from a Prussian map of the Oder Marshes, 1743.

Yet the changes that occurred from the mid-eighteenth century did represent something different. Earlier initiatives, whether undertaken by the Elector Joachim, the Great Elector, Frederick William I, or individual nobles, had been piecemeal. The new projects were more extensive, more comprehensive. The greater scale of the ambition matched the greater resources of the state. What was new in Frederick the Great's reign was not access to the all-important Dutch hydraulic specialists—the Great Elector and Frederick William I had also used Dutch engineers. What was novel was the growing expertise in land surveying, map-making, and statistics available to—and actively encouraged by—the absolutist ruler. This was an age of men like Johann Peter Süssmilch and Bernhard Ludwig Bekmann, who tabulated land, people, and raw materials or drew up detailed historical-geographical topographical surveys. This information put new power into the hands of rulers, making more ambitious projects thinkable. So, for example, whereas earlier efforts had tackled parts of the Oderbruch on a modest and piecemeal basis, the draining undertaken in the years 1747-53 followed a comprehensive plan that released some 150,000 acres for new uses.[6] Something similar was happening across Prussia, in the Warthebruch and Netzebruch, on the Dosse and Rhine, in the Wustrauer Luch, in the Drömling and the Madüe, on the island of Usedom. Reclamation projects led to the establishment of a thousand new villages or "colonies" that formed the largest single component of the 300,000 immigrants to Prussia during Frederick's reign.

These undertakings had many different motives. One of them was certainly the creation of new land on which colonists could be settled, part of the Frederician policy of peopling Prussia (*Peuplierungspolitik*). There was an ethnic dimension to this. German colonists would be planted in the Oderbruch where Wendish people had formerly fished, just as Germanization was an objective in newly acquired West Prussia, "a barbarous country sunk in ignorance and stupidity" dominated by the "slovenly Polish trash" (in Frederick the Great's words).[7] Reclaimed land would also increase the food supply to support a growing population. Early drainage projects in the Electoral March were intended to provision Berlin, the population of which grew from under 10,000 to well over 100,000 between 1680 and 1750, just as the Dutch drained inland lakes in the seventeenth century to feed Amsterdam.[8] At the same time, the cuts that altered the course of rivers like the Oder as part of the reclamation projects, forerunners of the great nineteenth-century schemes of Rhine "rectification," were intended to improve navigability and thereby aid commerce, as well as to prevent serious floods like the ones that had occurred in the Oderbruch nine times between 1698 and 1737.[9] Not least, drainage and reclamation projects were designed to secure Prussian state borders in the expanding eastern territories, for how could you protect or even define a frontier that was often underwater?

But there is something more. Running through these transformations, inseparably intertwined with them, is the motif of a tamed or conquered nature. Historians often quote from one of Frederick the Great's letters to Voltaire: "True riches consist only of that which comes out of the earth." The following sentence is just as important: "Whoever improves the soil, cultivates land lying waste and drains swamps, is making conquests from barbarism."[10] Conquests from barbarism—here was the authentic voice of eighteenth-century enlightened absolutism. Like other rulers of the time, Frederick sought (in Henning Eichberg's formulation) to "order, measure, discipline."[11] This applied to soldiers and subjects, to land and raw materials, to gardens, and to nature itself, where the Creator had left or dangerous or "barbarous" corners that served no "useful" purpose.

These opinions, commonplace among the educated, did not apply only to marshes and swamps. Drainage projects were mounted in parallel with three other notable efforts to master nature. One was the attempt to counter the shifting sand dunes on the North German Plain, which filled the air with fine particles that obscured roads and drifted on to fields, ruining standing crops. "With the exception of Libya, few states can boast of being our equal when it comes to sand," wrote Frederick sardonically.[12] A second was the campaign to control wildfires and the peasant practice of swiddening or fire farming (*Brandwirtschaft*), which state forestry officials considered dangerously irrational. Edicts on burning, the construction of fire-breaks, and more orderly planting of trees were among the methods pursued by enlightened officials who made Germany the undisputed European leader in scientific forestry.[13] Finally, these years saw the hunting to virtual extinction of bear, lynx, wolf, and other creatures, the culmination of a campaign that had begun after these species increased in numbers during the Thirty Years' War.[14] In fact, this was often linked by contemporaries to the draining of wetlands. Frederick, frustrated in the 1770s by the failure to eradicate wolves entirely in West Prussia, thought he knew where to place the blame and where to find the solution: "In order better to achieve the final objective, one must devise means of gradually draining the impenetrable marshes and bogs that house the wolves, making them accessible."[15] August Gottlob Meissner, who in 1782 wrote the first life of Franz Balthasar Schönberg von Brenckenhoff, perhaps the single most important agent of Frederician reclamation projects, recalled that before his hero's efforts "no plough had ever been here, no human industry had ever sought its fortune ... over an area of some miles one encountered nothing but swamp and dense undergrowth, the habitation of snakes and wolves."[16] Kammer-Rat Stubenrauch of the Order of St. John, which had major holdings in the Warthebruch, noted in 1787: "The whole region remained for a long time a dwelling place for wild animals, wolves, not infrequently bears, otters and other vermin (*Ungeziefer*) of every kind."[17]

The contemporary justification for human intervention of this kind was that man, "the lords and masters of nature" (in Descartes's words), the "master of the domain of earth" (in Buffon's), had a right and duty to "repair" or "improve" *natura lapsa*.[18] Perhaps on no other subject, however, was there such agreement as there was on the need to drain marshland. Whether we look at Buffon and Montesquieu in France, William Falconer and William Robertson in Britain, or Georg Forster and Immanuel Kant in Germany, the story is the same. Just as rulers and officials suspected marsh and fen as the breeding grounds of superstition and places that harboured disorderly human elements like deserters and bandits, so writers on natural history were agreed in viewing them as dark, disorderly corners of nature, where vegetation and animal bodies decayed, emitting noxious-smelling and unhealthy miasmas. The solution: to let in air and sunlight so that the recovered land could be put to use.[19]

We are dealing, in other words, with a self-conscious parallel to what was happening in the New World. It is no accident that new settlements in the Warthebruch bore confidently American names like Maryland, Florida, Philadelphia, and Charleston, to signify the arrival of a "superior" new culture.[20] But there is another parallel. The great drainage projects represented a real-life version of the great theme of mastery over nature that we find in *Faust*, Part II, where Faust eventually succeeds—at a price—in his great reclamation scheme aimed at "bringing the earth back to itself."[21] Historians need to find a way of writing about these events that avoids both a teleological account of progress or "modernization," and its declensionist mirror-image of lament for the world we have lost. One way to start is to pay close attention to the process as well as the outcome, to emphasize just how difficult it was to assert such mastery. For these changes were undeniably beset by countless difficulties. That is true whether we look at the large picture of reclamation schemes across Frederician Prussia, or examine individual projects at the micro level.

At the macro level, the obstacles included noble vested interest, the bureaucratic inertia of state officials and the General Directory, and the constant financial problems that led Frederick the Great to pen his notorious marginalia (*"non habeo pecuniam,"* "I haven't a *Groschen* to spare").[22] These obstacles led Frederick to cut corners by setting up special funds and appointing trouble-shooters with plenipotentiary powers to force through his projects, men like Brenkenhoff, the unlettered but energetic former war supplier from Anhalt-Dessau who was active mainly in the Prussian New March and Pomerania, Johann Friedrich Domhardt, another intensely practical man born outside Prussia, mainly active in the eastern provinces, and the engineer Simon Leonhard Haerlem, who was charged with seeing through the Oderbruch reclamation. Given the wide discretion they enjoyed and the pace at which they worked, it is hardly surprising that Frederick's plenipotentiaries themselves often cut corners. Some were financial (Brenkenhoff was a notorious offender); others left their traces on the completed—or half-completed—schemes.[23] The often desperately improvised character of these projects was a far cry from the image of the absolutist state machine. Political historians, of course, would hardly be surprised by this; historians of technology and the environment should keep it always at the forefront of their minds, for both groups have a tendency (although in quite opposite ways) to overestimate the smooth operation of that machine in effecting change.

When we turn up the magnification, the process of reshaping the land at the micro level closely resembled Murphy's Law: anything that can go wrong, will. Take the draining of the Lower Oderbruch as an example, for it was not untypical.[24] Three months after work began the supervising engineer died; he was followed to the grave two years later by the president of the Oderbruch Commission, which had overall responsibility for the undertaking. These were contingent misfortunes; other threats to the tempo of construction were more structural, and more serious. They included the outbreaks of fever that dogged the project, taking lives and causing serious illness among many more. This was marshy, malarial terrain, and the physically punishing nature of the work made the workers highly susceptible to illness. Despite contemporary advances in the science of hydraulic engineering and the quality of measuring instruments, the mechanical arts of construction still required the harnessing of basic energy sources. Carts and boats carried materials to the site, but it was human muscle power that did the rest, men standing waist-deep in water, wielding shovels, buckets and longhandled spades.

Figures 2 and 3. The arduous work of hydraulic improvements in eighteenth-century Prussia. From: David Gilly and Johann Albert Eytelwein, eds., *Praktische Anweisung zur Wasserbaukunst* (Berlin, 1802).

Illness made already serious labor shortages worse. Experienced dike-builders and canal-diggers were hard to come by and expensive; military service drained away laborers.[25] The slow rate of progress meant, in turn, that the project was more vulnerable to the elements—ice build-ups in winter and high water that breached half-completed dikes and led to flooding. An unreliable workforce, laboring in dreadful conditions and not always sure that it would be paid, also had to face non-cooperation and resistance from local inhabitants, who refused to provide the wood that made up the fascines needed for dike and embankment construction, withheld use of their boats to transport materials, and even drove cattle on to the new Oderdamm in an attempt to sabotage the scheme. That the initial phase of the Oderbruch improvement—making a cut in the river, and diking this stretch of the "New Oder"—was completed within six years was due mainly to use of the army. Two senior officers were sent in to speed up construction (the New Oder, or Petri Canal, was named after one of them), soldiers were drafted in as laborers, the site was placed under military guard, and recalcitrant locals were threatened with severe reprisals. Frederick the Great himself employed a military metaphor to describe the reclamation of the Oderbruch in his often quoted remark: "Here I have conquered a province in peace."[26] Later writers, such as Carl Heuer, would follow his lead. Whether the conquest was in fact so peaceful might be questioned. Contemporaries who referred to the construction project of 1746-53 as a "silently conducted Seven Years' War" were nearer the mark.[27] This arduous victory over natural and human forces of resistance depended on soldiers; violence was an essential part of the transformation.

Its results were ambiguous. The brave new world of dikes, ditches, windmills, fields and meadows did deliver many of the hoped-for benefits. New land was created for colonists, the food supply was increased. When Pastor Rehfeldt delivered the memorial oration at Brenkenhoff's funeral, he painted a picture of barren land transformed into "fields of joy and abundance."[28] And it is true that reclaimed land often proved exceptionally rich and productive, nowhere more so than the Oderbruch. As the soil dried out, the livestock raising of the early years was joined by a very diverse arable farming—rye, wheat, oats, barley, clover, and specialized cash crops.[29] Just as, to the east, Brenkenhoff planted vines in the hills between Küstrin and Bromberg, experimented with different varieties of lentils and peas, and filled the new land with Danish cattle, English sheep, Turkish goats and Don Cossack buffalo, so the Oderbruch provided almost laboratory conditions for the application of "improved" farming methods.[30] Here, in a newly organized landscape, the contemporary obsession with improved crops, rotations, and breeds (especially from England) could be put into practice. It could hardly be more fitting that a pioneer of scientific husbandry, Daniel Albrecht Thaer, should have settled there at Möglin in 1804, where he published the four volumes of his *Principles of Rational Agriculture*.[31] Nineteenth-century commentators, who so often looked down on the Oderbruch (as Frederick had always done) from the surrounding heights, invariably painted the same picture. This was a "blooming province" (Walter Christiani), a "green land in the sandy marches," "a large and beautiful garden"(Ernst Breitkreuz).[32]

Figure 4. "Frederick the Great views newly established colonies in the Rhinluch," oil painting by Johann Christoph Frisch (c.1800). From Christian Graf von Krockow and Karl-Heinz Jürgens, *Friedrich der Grosse Lebensbilder* (Bergisch Gladbach, 1986).

The Oderbruch also did well by its inhabitants: those, at any rate, who farmed and later owned the new land. By the third decade of the nineteenth century, the Oderbruch peasant had acquired a reputation for materialism and acquisitiveness that was striking even by prevailing standards of criticism on the part of officials, clergymen and other middle-class observers who found such wealth unseemly. The red-tiled and green-shuttered farmhouses, the carriages and finery, the consumption of tobacco and wines, the cards and skittles—these were the conventional symbols of vulgar prosperity. Few were more sardonic than Theodor Fontane, in the *Wanderungen durch die Mark Brandenburg* and novels such as *Unterm Birnbaum.* Yet Fontane, who knew the areas well from visiting his pharmacist father in Freienwalde, had no doubt that a "barren and worthless marshland" had been transformed into "the granary of our land."[33] The promise of a land of opportunity held out by Frederician colonist-recruiters, had apparently been redeemed. Life had imitated art, as the great reclamation of project in *Faust* was realized:

> Green are the meadows, fertile; and in mirth,
> Both men and herds live in this newest earth.[34]

And there was something more: malaria disappeared. Contemporaries may have had the wrong explanation when they associated malarial fevers with the "miasmas" that emanated from marshy regions, but they were not wrong to link the disease with marsh and fenland. With reclamation, malaria was no longer endemic across the North German Plain, disappearing as it had from the English fens a century earlier. Not only was standing water removed as a breeding ground. Where the new husbandry of livestock and dairy farming was practiced, it provided the malaria-carrying anopheles mosquito with a preferred source of blood; but the malarial plasmodium does not find cattle a suitable host, so the preference of this mosquito for cattle blood broke the chain of malaria transmission to humans.[35] The disappearance of malaria had far-reaching consequences. It meant the end of a disease that weakened the human immune system, making people less vulnerable to chronic diseases and infections. Like other by-products of the reclamations, it signalled the "end of the biological old regime," or at least the beginning of the end.[36]

It was benefits such as these—productive new land, increased food supply, the wiping out of malaria—that led the modern Dutch expert on reclamation Paul Wagret to refer in 1959 to "the conquest of marshlands by civilization."[37] It is harder today to summon such unqualified enthusiasm, for it is now more obvious that the benefits of conquest came at a price—human and environmental, short-term and long-term. Let me turn first to the human cost. There were people who stood in the way of Frederick's reclamations, just as the elderly couple Philomen and Baucis stood in the way of Faust's great project. Take the old Oderbruch, once again, as an example. It contained a thin scatter of villages built on higher sandy mounds. Their inhabitants—no more than 170 families directly in the Lower Marsh—were amphibious. They lived primarily as fishermen, from the rich stocks of carp, perch, pike, bream, barbel, ide, tench, lamprey, burbot, eel, and crabs. But they also produced hay and pastured animals when water-levels were lower, using the animal dung mixed with mud and bundles of twigs to construct protective walls against floods, and on those walls they grew vegetables, especially marrows. Except in winter, when ice provided an alternative, their principal means of communication through the labyrinthine waterways was by flat-bottomed boat. Even religious services consisted of a gathering of boats, when a pastor was rowed out from Wriezen on the edge of the marsh.[38]

This way of life was destroyed by the reclamation, but not without a struggle. The resistance echoed the stubbornness heard in the English Fens more than a century earlier:

> For they do mean all fens to drain
> And water overmaster
> All will be dry and we must die,
> 'cause Essex calves want pasture …
> We must give place (oh grievous case)
> To horned beast and cattle,
> Except that we can all agree
> To drive them out by battle.[39]

The Fens had witnessed riots and disorders; on the Oder, there were attempts to sabotage the work of reclamation, not only (as we have seen) during the initial stage of construction, but beyond. After the spring floods of 1754, Haerlem reported that breaches in the dikes "had been caused not only by the force of the water, but malicious inhabitants of the marsh, perhaps because of their fishing interest, had clandestinely pierced the dikes in three places and thereby caused major damage to the defenses."[40] The inhabitants of Old Mädewitz "offered resistance from their fortresses of marrows"—not, surely, the best of strategic positions.[41] Soldiers were once again deployed and offenders threatened with capital punishment.

Philomen and Baucis, having declined money and resettlement, were killed by Mephisto and his men when Faust lost patience. The former marsh-dwellers were offered, and most accepted, new land as compensation. Physical resistance ended; instead, fisher families used petitions and lawsuits to ensure that they received at least the compensation due to them, especially from noble and municipal landowners.[42] But there were plenty who clung defiantly, painfully, to a world that was disappearing, who found it impossible to exchange a fish-hook for a plough, although their children and grandchildren of course adapted (as we say) to the new regime of *terra firma*.

It is true that before the change these marsh-dwellers had hardly lived free from constraints. They owed a variety of seigneurial dues to their lords—money in lieu of labor service, a certain number of geese per year, "fish money," and so on. They also faced the monopoly power of the fish processors' guild (literally the

Hechtreisser, or pike-rippers' guild), whose members took their catches in Wriezen, then prepared and sold the fish.[43] The fisher people of the marsh may have lived in misty isolation, but they were part of a developed market economy as well as a surviving feudal system. And the harshness of their environment and a diet of "fish and crabs and crabs and fish" should certainly discourage any idealization, notwithstanding golden-age myths about extraordinary longevity.[44] On the other hand, their way of life was neither so irrational nor so abjectly vulnerable to the elements as officials and later writers often assumed. Their economy was carefully geared to the normal cycle of floods that occurred, before the reclamation, each spring and summer. Like the inhabitants of the Havelland and the east Münsterland recently examined by Rita Gudermann, they had evolved small-scale local solutions that permitted them to survive and fashion a livelihood from the waters until large-scale "improvements" came along. Gudermann's analysis has a good deal in common with the arguments developed in the recent book by James C. Scott, *Seeing Like a State: How Certain Schemes to Improve the Human Condition Have Failed*, a broad-brush critique of technological hubris and state power.[45] Scott also begins his account in eighteenth-century Prussia, although his focus is on forestry, not reclamation. Both authors are perhaps too impressed by the superiority of local customs and practical knowledge over the abstract plans of the improvers. But their narratives of avoidable error and loss record an important truth, and suggest one of the registers in which we should tell the history of a region like the Oderbruch.

It was not only the immediate inhabitants of the marshes whose former lives came to an end. The waters had supported fisher families from many surrounding towns and villages. With the disappearance of ponds, lakes and eel-weirs on the river they, too, had to seek a future elsewhere. Even the physical appearance of a town like Wriezen was transformed: "In places where the fishermen once cast their great nets one now sees meadows, even wheat and other kinds of corn."[46] As brewing and distilling flourished and Wriezen acquired a cattle show, the fishing business died, the old fish containers rotted, and abandoned boats turned into wrecks.

It was the colonists who represented the future. But the first generations of those colonists also paid a high price as they built the basis for later prosperity. The years-long projects on the Oder, Warthe, Netze, and elsewhere only created the preconditions for settlements—the cuts in the rivers, the major dikes, and embankments. The work of realizing them still had to be done by the incomers: ditching and diking the future grazing or arable land, pulling up the old vegetation and planting willows by the new drainage channels, preparing the still intractable soil, building paths and bridges, all the while trying to maintain the defenses against the water. Disease and heavy labor culled their ranks; many widows showed up in the "tables" of colonists compiled for Frederick the Great's scrutiny.[47] The original colonist houses, built too quickly on skimpy foundations, subsided and even collapsed. Animals died from infections after grazing on still water-logged meadows.[48] As the colonist saying went: "The first generation meets with death, the second with privation, only the third with prosperity."[49]

Figure 5.
The construction of a
new village: woodcut by
Vogel after Adolph von
Menzel, 1843-49. From
Galerie J.H. Bauer,
*Friedrich der Grosse
und seine Zeit. Bildnisse
und Darstellungen*
(Hanover, n.d.).

Some moved on, or returned home, like the luckless Herr Paulsen, who settled in the Oderbruch after Russian soldiers had destroyed his holding near
Landsberg on the Warthe during the Seven Years' War. In his first year at Neu-
Rüdnitz, he was robbed, and he and his wife assaulted, by a band of rampaging
Cossacks. In the second year, he lost fourteen head of cattle to disease and had
three horses stolen. In the third year, his fields were flooded, weeds ruined half his
crop, and a plague of mice ate the other half. In the fourth year, he was flooded
out again, losing all of his pigs and poultry. Then he sold up and went home.[50]

Of course, all settler or frontier societies have their stock of stories about epic
struggles, hard times, and hard-luck cases. In these stories the ones who fail to
"stick it out" have a important part, because they give a measure of the endurance
shown by those who did. Tales like these, worn smooth by the tellers, acquire a
timeless quality; but they seldom lose their sense of place, for that is what gives
them meaning, and in the hardships that befell German colonists we find important evidence about the costs of reclamation. Take those diseases and infections
of humans and livestock, or the infestations of mice and weeds. These were not
just bad luck, the vagaries of a cruel nature. Environmental historians have made
us familiar with the problems that arise when humans migrate from one ecosystem to another; for people carry their biota with them, in this case from every
part of the Holy Roman Empire and much of Europe beyond. To which we
must, of course, add the plants and animals introduced to the new land with
promiscuous zeal and mixed success. That some failed and others brought infections, or that some "servant species" (to use Alfred Crosby's term) got above
themselves, should cause us no surprise.[51]

Some of the familiar disasters of development were largely avoided on these
reclaimed lands. The rich alluvial soil (although not everywhere as rich as in the
Oderbruch) did not suffer the soil exhaustion found in some other marginal areas
brought into cultivation or used more intensively. Mixed farming helped, in
sharp contrast to the crisis that eventually overtook the monocropped German

pine forests. And a combination of climate and topography meant that soil erosion was not the problem it became in other parts of Germany or in the Great Plains of America.

There was, though, one obvious cause of erosion: the flooding that continued to overrun reclaimed marshes and low-lying valleys. For writers reluctant to give up metaphors of a vanquished enemy, periodic inundations were evidence of a powerful foe that still "rattled its chains mightily."[52] Major post-reclamation floods swept through the Oderbruch in 1754 and 1770, three times in the 1780s, including the catastrophic year 1785, in 1805, 1813, 1827, 1829, 1830, and twice more in the following decade, in 1843, 1854, 1868, twice in the 1870s, three times from 1888 to 1893, and so on into the twentieth century.[53] Both in the Oderbruch and elsewhere, the reasons were many. Either the work of reclamation was left incomplete (as it was at the western end of the Warthebruch); or older patterns asserted themselves (such as the "New Oder" silting up its bed, as the river had always done); or the improvement schemes had unforeseen consequences, as water squeezed out of one place returned in another, which happened almost everywhere to some degree. Sometimes, of course, whether in the 1750s or the 1940s, the reason was wartime neglect of the protective system.

The point that most deserves emphasis is that each major setback led to some kind of rethinking; and to study these well-intentioned responses one after the other is to be reminded very forcibly of something that historians know well about their work, but hydrological experts have found it harder to accept about theirs: that the state of the art is always provisional. Read the series of confident precriptions for the Oderbruch, and you find that each set of new measures promises *finally* to turn the trick and overcome the ignorance, or engineering mistakes, or political constraints, of earlier generations—right down to Werner Michalsky's claim in 1983 that under East German planning "the centuries-old dream of humanity to control the forces of nature has been realized under socialist conditions."[54]

The reality was that, taking the Oderbruch once again as an example, none of these supposedly definitive solutions—not the raising of dikes after the inundations of the 1770s, not blocking off the "Old Oder" following the major flood in 1830, not the large corrective scheme in the 1850s, not the advent of steam pumps and dredgers, not the new plan in the 1920s that used electrically powered pumps, not the repeated reorganizations of Dike Associations, not even socialist conditions—*none* of these was able to prevent floods that were now a threat to the work-cycle rather than a part of it.[55] Over a period of two centuries no definitive security against the water could be established in these reclaimed land. Instead, floods became less frequent but more catastrophic when they did occur, right down to the "once-in-a-century" flood of 1997, the second of its kind in fifty years.[56]

More than two hundred years later, it is also possible to gauge the environmental effects of eighteenth-century reclamation projects. Some of the impact was felt early and dramatically. A contemporary described what happened after the rooting up of the old, tangled undergrowth of the Oderbruch. Left in huge piles for months to dry out, it became a refuge for wildlife of every kind. Then, when light was finally set to the piles, the wildlife fled the fire and smoke, an easy prey—wild cats, weasels, martens, foxes, wolves, deer, hares, wild ducks, fen chickens. Theodor Fontane, who later recalled the incident in his *Wanderungen,* called it a "war of extermination" (*Vernichtungskrieg*).[57] But the damage done by blazing guns was much less significant over time than the loss of a diverse habitat. These had been rich wetlands, a complex ecosystem of land and water, trees, bushes, reeds, and trailing lianas that supported a now almost unimaginable range of insect, fish, bird, and animal life.

We have some striking contemporary accounts of what such areas looked like before reclamation. The Havelland marsh had been "a savage, primitive land, as the hand of nature had created it, a counterpart to the primeval forests of South America." As for the old Warthebruch, "anyone who had dared to enter it would have felt himself transposed to one of the most unknown parts of the world." A Danish traveller compared the already reclaimed parts of the Warthebruch—whose "beauty" was "like paradise"—with the "Canadian wildnerness" that still remained untouched.[58] His comparison reminds us that we have to read such commentators against the grain, for these were men who deplored the unimproved marshlands. But other voices in the late eighteenth century were already sounding a different note, some of them drawing on the evidence of the New World to warn that nature could not be "mastered by force."[59] These were the naturalists, travellers, nature poets, and disciples of Jean-Jacques Rousseau who formed the first "green wave" in German culture that culminated in the 1770s.[60] The Romantics followed, lamenting the fact that human domination had (as Novalis put it) "made the eternal creative music of the universe into the monotonous clapping of a monstrous mill."[61] As the eighteenth century gave way to the nineteenth, and the nineteenth to the twentieth, these voices grew in volume; the earlier "discovery" of mountains and seashore was joined by a new appreciation for precious but precarious areas of heath, marsh and fen; and the history of German wetlands came to be related more critically, with a greater emphasis on the flora and fauna that had been so carelessly sacrificed. The development of ornithology and a strong German bird-protection movement was just one telling sign of shifting sentiment. A sharper eye was turned to losses as well as gains, including under the former the "monotony" often touched on by Fontane.[62] By the time we get to a pessimistic, ecologically minded writer in the 1950s like Hans Künkel, whose ancestors came from both the Oderbruch and Warthebruch, that Danish traveller's scale of values has been reversed. It is no longer the reclaimed land that is a paradise, but the wetlands in their pristine state: "A paradise of creatures great and small, and especially of birds."[63] A paradise lost, in other words.

There is certainly no denying the magnitude or destructive power of the human impact on the natural world of the eighteenth century. This occurred before the fossil fuel-based era of industrialization, and in the wetlands of the

North German Plain it led to a devastating loss of biodiversity. Two hundred and fifty years on from the great reclamation project in the Oderbruch, efforts are now being made to "renature" the area and others like it. It is no more misleading to view the original transformation in terms of a "paradise lost" than it is to speak of a "conquest of marshlands by civilization." It is no more misleading; but it is just *as* misleading.

A lost paradise, whether or not the term itself is used, rests on the idea of a distinct before-and-after. The natural world is stable, harmonious and self-equilibriating; the human impact brings instability, disharmony and disequilibrium. When environmental historians and other writers argue for a break of this kind, they are following the impulse of the Romantics, whose holistic categories did so much to tinge modern ecological thinking. The trouble is that arguments like these have been seriously challenged by modern ecologists, who emphasize instead the the disturbance-dependence of species and the unstable dynamism of nature. Chaos theory has dislodged comfortable organic metaphors. When a prominent environmental historian like Donald Worster tell us that "nature, left alone, demonstrates a marvellous system of organization," he is therefore recycling arguments that are widely discredited among ecologists themselves—hardly unprecedented, it is true, when historians borrow from other disciplines.[64]

When we look at these apparently pristine Prussian habitats, the "before" of the before-and-after, another question arises. How pristine were they? Was this really (to recall that earlier commentator) a "land created by the hand of nature"? The answer is: not really. Within both distant and fairly recent historical time the land had been repeatedly shaped and reshaped, even if less dramatically than it was to be in the reign of Frederick the Great. The reclamation projects themselves often turned up signs of early human settlements, but we do not even have to go that far back. There is evidence that just 500 years earlier there had been settlements in subsequently impenetrable marshlands, until a combination of climatic change and human actions led to catastrophic floods that drove them to higher ground.[65] It was in the following centuries that fisher people and hunter-gatherers developed their own micro-economies in areas like the Oderbruch and Warthebruch. They, in turn, placed their stamp on the land, hunters not least. There is probably no better depiction of the ecological old regime than Jan Brueghel the Elder's "Interior of the Woods with Huntsman"; but as our eyes are drawn into the scene, we can hardly miss the point that without the huntsman there would be no picture of this wooded waterland in the first place.[66] And the same goes for the wildlife within it. The 3,000-strong herd of deer reported from the seventeenth-century Warthebruch owed as much to the hand of man as the hand of nature.[67] In fact, almost all of the areas I have been talking about were hunting preserves before they became pastures or fields of corn, which is why so many Prussian nobles also protested the process of reclamation.

Examine these apparently natural habitats closely, and it becomes apparent just how much they owed to human actions. Those high water levels were sometimes high because they had been raised by the operation of nearby mills.[68] The hydrology of lowland marshes was affected by the adaptation of upland streams for wood rafting or to power hammer mills. Alluvial deposits occurred in flood-prone river valleys because of topsoil erosion caused by deforestation in distant uplands.[69] There is, in fact, no obvious baseline for measuring the world that was "lost." If, as I suggested earlier, the great illusion of the progress-mongers and "modernizers" has been the belief that *this* time there was a once-for-all, definitive solution, the equal and opposite snare for the ecologically minded has been to believe in a once-for-all state of nature. To quote Elizabeth Ann Bird, however, it is possible to "argue against environmentally destructive technologies, but not on the grounds that they are anti-natural."[70]

Of course there is a natural world of climate, soils, waters, vegetation, disease, and animals. But we know this nature (*Natur an sich*, for German writers) at second hand, through the lenses of our beliefs, cultures and structures of knowledge.[71] We could not "think like a river"—Donald Worster again—even if we wanted to.[72] I noted earlier how often those who described the Oderbruch literally looked down on it from above, just like the unknown artist who produced a seventeenth-century engraving of the Zehden marshes in the style of Matthäus Merian. This neatly symbolizes the historian's problem of perspective. We are like Theodor Fontane, bitter-sweetly recording the "declining power" or "loss of character," yet forever framing a kind of panorama.[73] Much of what we know about the object of our attention also, paradoxically, presupposes communications that heralded its demise. The lost marshlands were never so familiar as when they were disappearing. A notable example of this perspectival problem is that great friend of the moors, the Worpswede painter Otto Modersohn. He confided to his diary that "nature is our teacher," then noted that he had this not very original thought "on the bridge that leads over the canal."[74]

Let me offer a few concluding remarks that place the arguments of this essay within two larger contexts. First, the history of human interaction with the natural world deserves a larger place in mainstream history. This approach faces special problems of acceptance in the case of German history. It is not just that more conservative scholars are indifferent or hostile to the environmental perspective. Others are nervous of the implications. There is concern that "anti-modernism" lies behind green-tinged history, as well as a deeper anxiety triggered by negative associations with the crude environmental determinism that was so influential in the 1920s and 1930s. The second of these concerns is surely unfounded; the first is more complex, because even many of those (including myself) who see a powerful destructive potential in "modernism" would recognize that sentimentality poses a genuine problem when it comes to writing about the environment—a tendency to view nature as a separate and purer realm, a victim. In both cases, however, the issues need to be faced. If the environmental perspective is to become part of German mainstream history, those cultural and political questions cannot be ducked. In the United States, after all, the "New Western History" has helped to recast our understanding of the American past—of American history as a whole—by addressing questions like these, not by avoiding them.

Secondly, in the era after the "linguistic turn" it is important to defend the legitimacy of a materialist history. Sometimes, reading yet another book or article on another "imagined place," it is tempting to echo Gertrude Stein and complain that "there's no *there* there." This should not be misconstrued as a plea to turn our backs on the cultural and political meanings attached to the physical landscape. Quite the contrary. If environmental history is to have an impact on mainstream history, it must also concern itself with mental geographies and the constructs that humans place on the natural world. Nature—"perhaps the most complex word in the language," as Raymond Williams called it—is a nodal point where the environmental, economic, social, political and cultural come together.[75]

This essay has told two intertwined histories. One concerns the physical transformation that occurred across the wetlands of the North German Plain in the second half of the eighteenth century. It was a dramatic chapter in the history of human intervention in the natural world, with many destructive effects on ecological diversity and complex implications, both long-term and short-term, benign and less benign, on the human inhabitants of the region. The second history is one of power and perceptions—who drained the land, who resisted it, what hopes and fears were bound up with the outcome? The alchemy that turned water into land in Frederician Prussia indicates where the lines of power ran in the late absolutist state, and how human sentiments were projected on to nature, whether to "conquer" or to "save" it. These histories were not separated; and the more we are able to reflect that fact when we write about them, the better. Christof Dipper's fine history of Germany from 1648 to 1789 has a pair of neatly twinned chapters—*Die Herrschaft der Natur, Die Natur der Herrschaft.*[76] To paraphrase him: by understanding the human dominance of nature, we have much to learn about the nature of human dominance.

Notes

1. Jon Krakauer, *Into Thin Air* (New York, 1997); Sebastian Junger, *The Perfect Storm* (New York, 1997); Erik Larson, *Issac's Storm: A Man, a Time, and the Deadliest Hurricane in History* (New York, 1999). I am quoting from the excerpt in *Time*, Aug. 30, 1999.
2. Christoph Ransmayr, *Die Schrecken des Eises und der Finsternis* (Vienna, 1984).
3. Walter Christiani, *Das Oderbruch. Historische Skizze* (Freienwalde a. 0., 1901), Anhang II. The original reads:

> Der überwund'ne Mächtige
> Ist unser Oderstrom
> Und sein Gebiet das Oderbruch;
> Der Held, der ihn in Fesseln schlug,
> Stieg auf zum Himmelsdom.
> Zwar regt sich wieder jetzt der Feind

Und droht mit neuem Krieg;
Doch da von Vater Fritzens Thron
Sein hoher Geist nicht ist entfloh'n,
So winkt uns neuer Sieg

4. See David Blackbourn, *A Sense of Place: New Directions in German History.* The 1998 Annual Lecture of the German Historical Institute London (London, 1999).
5. Hermann Kellenbenz, *Deutsche Wirtschaftsgeschichte,* 2 vols. (Munich, 1977-81), 1: 233; Max Beheim-Schwarzbach, *Hohenzollernsche Colonisationen,* (Leipzig, 1874), 1-95.
6. On the reclamation of the Oderbruch, in addition to Christiani, *Oderbruch* and Beheim-Schwarzbach, *Colonisationen,* see Theodor Fontane, *Wanderungen durch die Mark Brandenburg,* Hanser Verlag edition, 3 vols. (Munich and Vienna, 1991), 1: 550-88; Heinrich Berger, *Friedrich der Grosse als Kolonisator* (Giessen, 1896); Albert Detto, "Die Besiedlung des Oderbruches durch Friedrich den Grossen," *Forschungen zur Brandenburgischen und Preussischen Geschichte* 16 (1903): 163-72; Ernst Breitkreutz, *Das Oderbruch im Wandel der Zeit* (Remscheid, 1911); Peter Fritz Mengel, ed., *Das Oderbruch,* 2 vols. (Eberswalde, 1930-34); Berndt Herrmann, with Martina Kaup, *"Nun Blüht es von End' zu End' überall." Die Eindeichung des Nieder-Oderbruches 1747-1753* (Münster, 1997).
7. Berger, *Friedrich der Grosse als Kolonisator,* 54; Reinhold Koser, *Geschichte Friedrichs des Grossen,* 3 vols. (Darmstadt, 1974), 3:351. The verb in the first of these quotations was *"croupir"*, with its undertones of wallowing or stagnating. Note also Frederick's comment on the "stupidity and savagery" of Upper Silesian Poles: Beheim-Schwarzbach, *Hohenzollernsche Colonisationen,* 271.
8. Jan Peters, Hartmut Harnisch, and Lieselott Enders, *Märkische Bauerntagebücher des 18. und 19. Jahrhunderts* (Weimar, 1989), 39-40.
9. Heinrich Berghaus, *Landbuch der Mark Brandenburg und des Markgrafthums Nieder-Lausitz,* 3 vols. (Brandenburg 1854-56) 3: 27 (table 8). In the nearby Warthebruch a "major flood" had occurred about every tenth year since 1500: Erich Neuhaus, *Die Fridericianische Colonisation im Netze- und Warthebruch* (Landsberg, 1905), 28-9.
10. Beheim-Schwarzbach, *Hohenzollernsche Colonisationen,* 266.
11. Henning Eichberg, "Ordnen, Messen, Disziplinieren: Moderner Herrschaftsstaat und Fortifikation," in Johannes Kunisch, ed., *Staatsverfassung und Heeresverfassung in der europäischen Geschichte der frühen Neuzeit* (Berlin, 1986), 347-75.
12. Frederick the Great to Voltaire, Jan. 10, 1776: Rudolph Stadelmann, *Preussens Könige in ihrer Thätigkeit für die Landescultur,* 4 vols.(Leipzig, 1878-87) 2:43.
13. Stephen Pyne, *Vestal Fire. An Environmental History, Told Through Fire, of Europe and Europe's Encounter with the World* (Seattle, 1997), 147, 178-88, 203.
14. Henry Makowski and Bernhard Buderath, *Die Natur dem Menschen untertan* (Munich, 1983), 132.
15. Decree of June 7, 1776: Stadelmann, *Preussens Könige,* 2:81.
16. August Gottlob Meissner, *Leben Franz Balthasar Schönberg von Brenkenhof, Königl. Preuss. geheim. Ober-Finanz-Kriegs- und Domainenrath* (Leipzig, 1782), 80-1.
17. Neuhaus, *Fridericianische Colonisation,* 8-9.
18. Rene Descartes, *Discourse on Method and Related Writings,* translated by Desmond M. Clarke (Harmondsworth, 1999), 44; Georges-Louis Leclerc, Comte de Buffon, *Histoire Naturelle,* 44 vols. (Paris, 1749-1804) 12:14.
19. Clarence Glacken, *Traces on the Rhodian Shore: Nature and Culture in Western Thought from Ancient Times to the End of the Eighteenth Century* (Berkeley, 1967), 577, 604-6, 663-5, 670, 702-3; Yi-Fu Tuan, *Passing Strange and Wonderful: Aesthetics, Nature and Culture* (Washington, D.C., 1993), 61.
20. Otto Kaplick, *Das Warthebruch. Eine deutsche Kulturlandschaft im Osten* (Würzburg, 1956), 23-5.

21. Johann Wolfgang von Goethe, *Faust*, Part II, lines 10, 218-11, 580. See also Gerhard Kaiser, "Vision und Kritik der Moderne in Goethes *Faust* II," in *Merkur* 48/7 (July 1994): 594-604; Marshall Berman, *All That Is Solid Melts Into Air* (New York, 1982), 41-86.

22. Beheim-Schwarzbach, *Hohenzollernsche Colonisationen*, 275.

23. On these special assignments (*Sonderaufträge*) and the "improvised" aspect of reclamation projects, see Benno von Knobelsdorff-Brenkenhoff, *Eine Provinz im Frieden Erobert. Brenkenhoff als Leiter des friderizianischen Retablissements in Pommern 1762-1780* (Cologne and Berlin, 1984); Koser, *Geschichte*, 3:342-3; Ulrike Müller-Weil, *Absolutismus und Aussenpolitik in Preussen* (Stuttgart, 1992), 262-81.

24. See note 6 for sources.

25. On the specialist *Teichgrabers* of the eighteenth century, see Ludwig Hempel, "Zur Entwicklung der Kulturlandschaft in Bruchländereien," *Berichte zur deutschen Landeskunde* 11 (1952): 73; on rising hourly rates in this part of Prussia, Neuhaus, *Fridericianische Colonisation*, 39-40.

26. Christiani, *Oderbruch*, 46; Koser, *Geschichte*, 3:97.

27. Fontane, *Wanderungen*, 1:570.

28. Dr. Rehmann, "Kleine Beiträge zur Charakteristik Brenkenhoffs," *Schriften des Vereins für Geschichte der Neumark* 22 (1908): 115.

29. Christiani, *Oderbruch*, 92-100.

30. P. Schwarz, "Brenkenhoffs Berichte über seine Tätigkeit in der Neumark," *Schriften des Vereins für Geschichte der Neumark* 20 (1907): 37-101.

31. The first volume of *Grundsätze der rationellen Landwirtschaft* appeared in 1809, volumes 2-4 in 1810-12. In 1806, Möglin became the home of Germany's first academic institution for scientific agriculture.

32. Christiani, *Oderbruch*, preface; Breitkreutz, *Oderbruch*, iii, 116. On the "blooming garden" of the Warthebruch, see Hans Künkel, *Auf den kargen Hügeln der Neumark* (Würzburg, 1962), 32.

33. Fontane, *Wanderungen*, 1: 559-60. There is a similarly lyrical description in the novel *Vor dem Sturm* (*Before the Storm*, 1878), where the picture of plenty is transposed to the period of the Napoleonic wars: "The fruitfulness of this virgin soil moved the heart to a feeling of joyful gratitude, such as the Patriarchs may have felt when, in regions empty of men, they numbered the God-given yield of their house and their herds." *Before the Storm*, edited by R. J. Hollingdale (Oxford, 1985), 123-24.

34. Goethe, *Faust*, II, lines 11,563-4.

35. William McNeill, *Plaques and Peoples* (Garden City, 1976), 218.

36. See Fernand Braudel, *Capitalism and Material Life 1400-1800*, (London, 1974), 37-54.

37. Paul Wagret, *Polderlands* (London, 1968), 45.

38. Fontane, *Wanderungen*, 1: 574-81, which—like most later accounts—draws on Pastor S. Buchholz, *Versuch einer Geschichte der Churmark Brandenburg*, 2 vols. (Berlin, 1765), written just as. things were changing.

39. Fred Pearce, *The Dammed* (London, 1992), 32-3.

40. Breitkreutz, *Oderbruch*, 14-15.

41. Künkel, *Auf den kargen Hügeln*, 54.

42. Detto, "Besiedlung," 198-200.

43. F. W. Noeldechen, *Oekonomische und staatswissenschaftliche Briefe über das Niederoderbruch und den Abbau oder die Verteilung der Königliche Amter und Vorwerke im hohen Oderbruch* (Berlin, 1800), 69, on seigneurial obligations; Rudolf Schmidt, *Wriezen*, 2 vols. (Bad Freienwalde, 1931-32), 2: 20, on the guild.

44. Fontane, *Wanderungen*, 3: 578.

45. Rita Gudermann, *Morastwelt und Paradies: Ökonomie und Ökologie in der Landwirtschaft am Beispiel der Meliorationen in Westfalen und Brandenburg (1830-1880)* (Paderborn, 2000); James J. Scott, *Seeing Like a State: How Certain Schemes to Improve the Human Condition Have Failed* (New Haven, 1998).

46. Schmidt, *Wriezen*, 2: 21.

47. Siegfried Maire, "Beiträge zur Besiedlungsgeschichte des Oderbruchs," *Archiv der 'Brandenburgia' Gesellschaft für Heimatkunde der Provinz Brandenburg* 13 (1911): 21-160.

48. Breitkreutz, *Oderbruch*, 36; W. O. Henderson, *Studies in the Economic Policy of Frederick the Great* (London, 1963), 82; Schwarz, "Brenkenhoffs Berichte," 60; Knebelsdorff-Brenkenhoff, *Eine Provinz im Frieden Erobert*, 86.

49. "Die ersten haben den Tod, die zweiten die Not, die dritten das Brot": Peters, Harnisch, Enders, *Märkische Bauertagebücher*, 53.

50. Breitkreutz, *Oderbruch*, 87-8.

51. Alfred Crosby, *Ecological Imperialism: The Biological Expansion of Europe, 900-1900* (Cambridge, 1986), 22.

52. Breitkreutz, *Oderbruch*, 117.

53. Christiani, *Oderbruch*, 49-66; Koser, *Geschichte*, 3: 200-1. Maire, "Beiträge," has a good microhistorical account of what this meant for colonists on the Oderbruch villages of Vevais and Beauregard.

54. Werner Michalsky, *Zur Geschichte des Oderbruchs. Die Entwässerung* (Seelow, 1983), 12.

55. See *Die Melioration der Ueberschwemmung ausgesetzten Theile des Nieder- und Mittel-Oderbruchs* (Berlin, 1847); Wehrmann, *Die Eindeichung des Oderbruches* (Berlin, 1861); Christiani, *Oderbruch*, 49-81; Hans-Peter Trömel, *Deichverbände im Oderbruch* (Bad Freienwalde, 1988).

56. Severe flooding occurred exactly fifty years earlier, in 1947.

57. Fontane, *Wanderungen*, 1: 585.

58. Fontane, *Wanderungen*, 2: 104-5 (citing Klöden); Neuhaus, *Fridericianische Colonisation*, 8-9 (citing Stubenrauch); Künkel, *Auf den kargen Hügeln*, 33.

59. Glacken, *Traces*, 541-2, which also notes the German influence of the Swedish naturalist Peter Kalm, who pointed to changing climate and reduced numbers of fish and birds where swamps had been cleared in North America, urging his own countrymen not to be "blind to the future."

60. Henning Eichberg, "Stimmung über Heide - vom romantischen Blick zur Kolonisierung des Raumes," in Götz Großklaus and Ernst Oldemeyer, eds., *Natur als Gegenwelt: Beiträge zur Kulturgeschichte der Natur* (Karlsruhe, 1983), 217; see also Jost Hermand, *Grüne Utopien in Deutschland: Zur Geschichte des ökologischen Bewußtseins* (Frankfurt am Main, 1991), 32-8.

61. Rolf Peter Sieferle, *Fortschrittsfeinde? Opposition gegen Technik und Industrie von der Romantik bis zur Gegenwart* (Munich, 1984), 46.

62. Fontane, *Wanderungen*, 1: 593 (on the Oderbruch); and 2: 101-2 (on the Havelland).

63. Künkel, *Auf den kargen Hügel*, 51.

64. Donald Worster, in a review of William Cronon's *Changes in the Land*, in *Agricultural History* 58 (1984): 508-9. For criticism of Worster, and the changes in ecological thinking, see David Demeritt, "Ecology, Objectivity and Critique in Writings on Nature and Human Society," *Journal of Historical Geography* 20 (1994): 22-37; William Cronon, "The Uses of Environmental History," *Environmental History Review* 17 (1993): 1-22.

65. T. Dunin-Wasowicz, "Natural Environment and Human Settlement over the Central European Lowland in the 13th Century," in Peter Brindlecombe and Christian Pfister, eds., *The Silent Countdown. Essays in European Environmental History* (Berlin and Heidelberg, 1990), 90-105.

66. The picture is reproduced in Makowski and Buderath, *Natur*, 158.

67. Neuhaus, *Fridericianische Colonisation*, 4.

68. Bruno Krüger, *Die Kietzsiedlungen in Nördlichen Mitteleuropa* (Berlin, 1962), 109. Peters, Harnisch and Enders, *Märkische Bauerntagebücher*, 24, describe earlier conflicts between millers and reclamation engineers. The raising of water-levels as a result of millers' activities was a major problem during the reclamation work on the Madüe: Knobelsdorff-Brenkenhoff, *Eine Provinz im Frieden Erobert*, 88-148.

69. Makowski and Buderath, *Natur*, 172-3; Glacken, *Traces*, 698-702.

70. Elizabeth Ann Bird, "The Social Construction of Nature," *Environmental Review* 11 (1987): 261.

71. In addition to Großklaus and Oldemeyer, eds., *Natur als Gegenwelt,* see Ruth Groh and Dieter Groh, *Weltbild und Naturaneignung: Zur Kulturgeschichte der Natur* (Frankfurt am Main, 1991) and *Die Außenwelt der Innenwelt: Kulturgeschichte der Natur 2* (Frankfurt am Main, 1996).

72. Donald Worster, *The Wealth of Nature* (New York and Oxford, 1993), 123-34 ("Thinking Like a River").

73. Fontane, *Wanderungen,* 2: 108-9 (on the Brieselang).

74. Makowski and Buderath, *Natur,* 226.

75. Raymond Williams, *Keywords* (Glasgow, 1976), 184.

76. Christof Dipper, *Deutsche Geschichte 1648-1789* (Frankfurt am Main, 1991), chaps. I and V.

Chapter 2

THE POLITICAL ECOLOGY OF THE RHINE

Mark Cioc

"Anyone who wishes to speak about the Rhine," wrote the French historian Marc Bloch in 1933, "must first exorcise the demons—the myths, passions, and mental images—that bedevil our ability to decipher its past."[1] Writing as Adolf Hitler came to power in Germany with the goal of creating a Nazi Rhine as a prelude to a Nazi Europe, Bloch had French and German river myths uppermost in his mind. But his warning is applicable more generally, for even today our mental maps of the Rhine are clouded in myths and misconceptions. This essay will focus on three of the most common ones: the myth of national ownership, the myth of a Romantic river, and the myth of ecological restoration.[2]

It was the first myth—the myth of national ownership—that troubled Bloch. He understood better than did most of his contemporaries that the bloodshed between Germany and France would never cease so long as the nationalist myth-makers were left unchallenged. Historically, the Rhine has been (and remains today) an international river in every sense of the word. For well over two millennia, its watershed has not come under the exclusive control of any ethnic or linguistic group, at least not long enough to put anything remotely like a distinct national stamp on it. In *Commentarii de bello Gallico*, the oldest known book with a description of the Rhine, Julius Caesar noted that the river flows "through the territories of the Nantuates, Helvetii, Sequani, Mediomatrices, Triboci, and Treveri."[3] The names and ethnic groupings have changed over time—today they are Switzerland, Liechtenstein, Austria, Germany, France, Luxembourg, Belgium, and the Netherlands—but the river's multi-ethnic and multi-national character has remained remarkably constant.

Four contemporary states—Switzerland, the Netherlands, Germany, and France—are central to the Rhine's political ecology today. The "Swiss Rhine" includes almost the entire headwaters—chiefly the Alpenrhein and Aare tributary systems—which collectively account for about half of the river's annual volume of water. At the other end of the river is the "Dutch Rhine," which for all intents and purposes is synonymous with the delta. All of the river's water, sediment, and pollutants ultimately land in the Netherlands or get washed into the North Sea at Hoek van Holland, just downstream from Rotterdam. Between Switzerland and the Netherlands lies what can loosely be called the "German Rhine," which includes about 100,000 square kilometers of the river's watershed, representing slightly over half its total catchment area of 185,000 square kilometers.[4] German-speaking peoples have for centuries been most numerous in the Rhine basin and also the controllers of the lion's share of the Rhine's major non-Alpine tributaries: the Neckar, Main, Mosel, Wupper, Ruhr, Erft, Emscher, and Lippe.

The "French Rhine" is a more complicated matter, politically and geographically. France is the newest of the modern Rhine powers (leaving aside the myth of continuity between ancient Rome and modern France). Its direct geographic connection to the Rhine began in the late seventeenth century, when Louis XIV seized Strasbourg and other Alsatian cities as part of a military campaign to extend France's eastern frontier (to use Cardinal Richelieu's famous phrase) "jusqu'au Rhin."[5] From then on, France's Rhine possessions waxed and waned with France's military fortunes in Europe. Today the "French Rhine" consists of Alsace and Lorraine, the two geographically small (but symbolically huge) left-bank provinces that caused the Rhine to run red for so many centuries. France, however, played a far greater role in the creation of the modern Rhine than its belated appearance as a riparian power and its small geographic conquests might suggest.

Two points need emphasis here. First, the Rhine as a geographic space is not synonymous with Alsace and Lorraine, French and German mythmakers notwithstanding. The river has never functioned well as a political, economic, linguistic, or cultural frontier, despite a centuries-long attempt by the French to make it one. The Rhine's total length is 1,250 kilometers as measured from its Alpenrhein headwaters above Lake Constance to its mouth at Hoek van Holland. Only around 350 kilometers now serves as a national border, and most of that border separates Switzerland from its three riparian neighbors: Liechtenstein, Austria, and Germany. A scant 125 kilometers—only one-tenth of its total length—separates Alsace (France) and Baden (Germany) in the stretch between Basel and Strasbourg. Second, the Rhine is not and never has been "Germany's river, not Germany's border," the rhetoric of Ernst Moritz Arndt and other nineteenth-century German patriots to the contrary.[6] Locked as they were in a long political and military struggle with France, the Germans tended to see the Rhine solely through an east-west mindset, thereby overlooking the centrality of Switzerland in the south and the Netherlands in the north to the river's political and ecological affairs.

A third point, often overlooked, needs to be highlighted as well. Just a short time after Arndt declared the Rhine to be "Germany's river" in 1813, European diplomats meeting at the Vienna Congress (1814-15) drew a different conclusion and embarked on one of the greatest experiments of the nineteenth century: the internationalization of the Rhine as a commercial waterway and the establishment of a free-trade zone along its banks. These ideas were codified in Article 5 of the 1814 Paris Peace Treaty and Articles 108-116 of the Vienna Final Acts of 1815, and they were warmly supported by the Prussian diplomat Wilhelm von Humboldt, the Austrian diplomat Clemens von Metternich, the French and Dutch delegations, and all of the German riparian states.[7] By declaring the Rhine to be an "international" river and bringing it under an international "regime," diplomats sought to realize the important economic goal of removing the river's main commercial choke points—chiefly toll booths and dangerous cliffs—that had hindered trade for centuries. And they backed up their declaration by establishing (albeit with some time lag) the Central Commission for Rhine Navigation. It was the first ever river commission in Europe and it served as a model for subsequent commissions on the Elbe (1821), Weser (1823), Ems (1853), Danube (1856), and elsewhere. Headquartered in Strasbourg, the Rhine Navigation Commission lays claim to being the oldest continuous transnational institution in Europe and the first step in the long chain of events that led to the Common Market and European Union.

Here the French contribution needs highlighting, for the Vienna Congress' accomplishments did not occur in a political vacuum. Bourbon France had been pushing to internationalize the Rhine since the Peace of Westphalia (1648), and French revolutionaries finally realized this longstanding goal when they poured across the river at the end of the eighteenth century. "The restrictions and obstacles formerly placed on Rhine sailing and trading directly conflict with natural law, to which all Frenchmen are sworn to uphold," stated the French Executive Council decree of November 1792. "The flow of rivers is a common asset, not given to transfer or sale, of all states whose waters feed them."[8] The Vienna diplomats excised the references to natural law, but otherwise let the French achievement stand: "Navigation on the Rhine, from the point where it becomes navigable to the sea and vice versa, shall be free, in that it cannot be prohibited to any one."[9]

On other matters, too, the French legacy was immense. The Rhine Navigation Commission was prefigured by the Magistrat du Rhin, a Napoleonic agency created in 1808 to handle France's commercial and engineering matters on the river. Without altering its fundamental goals, the Vienna Congress simply restructured the commission as an international rather than French-dominated body. The territorial impact was also enormous. The French Revolution swept away the political structure that had prevailed on the Rhine since medieval times, replacing the ancien régime of German lilliputian states and principalities with modern middle-sized Napoleonic creations—Baden, Württemberg, Hessen, Nassau, Berg, and Westphalia—all under the aegis of the Rhine Confederation (1806-13). After Napoleon's defeat in 1815, the Vienna delegates simply accepted these states as legitimate, thus leaving intact a group of German riparian powers large enough to participate in full-scale engineering work on the river.

The Rhine Navigation Commission acted as a powerful tool for constructing an international river—not a German or French one—in the nineteenth and twentieth centuries. There were, to be sure, plenty of bumps along the way. European diplomats had to revisit Rhine political and economic affairs in 1831 (Mainz Acts), again in 1868 (Mannheim Acts), and again in 1919 (Versailles Treaty). But each new agreement strengthened rather than diluted the spirit of cooperation encoded in the original Vienna accords. Nineteenth-century nationalists notwithstanding, modern Rhine affairs largely came into the hands of like-minded Eurocrats and Euro-engineers who worked with the Rhine Navigation Commission and with each other. This cooperative spirit ensured a level of coherence to Rhine engineering projects and guaranteed a degree of intra-European cooperation that was otherwise out of step with European affairs in general and with German-French relations in particular. Not always, of course. The Germans were slow to rectify the stretch between Basel and Mannheim in the late nineteenth century because the Baden government profited handsomely from the railroad lines there. In the 1920s, the French began construction of the Grand Canal d'Alsace in order to make Strasbourg a major Rhine port, even though it negatively impacted the water table in Baden. But these were the exceptions, not the rule.

What is most remarkable about the Rhine Commission is how much it managed to accomplish, even though it was a purely advisory board, had no mechanisms of enforcement, and required the unanimous approval of its member states before it could act. The commission was successful mostly because the issues that came before it have been of common concern, making its recommendations hard to ignore or thwart outright. The commission took the lead in standardizing navigational regulations, police ordinances, and emergency procedures on the river. It oversaw the difficult transition from the age of rafts and sailboats to the age of steamers, diesels, and push-tows. It initiated regulations on the transport of hazardous materials and the like. Almost all blueprints—from a simple bridge construction to elaborate engineering projects—passed through the commission's offices for approval before work commenced. Nationalism played havoc with the Rhine Commission on occasion, mostly during wartime; but the commission itself thought and planned broadly in terms of Europe and not narrowly in terms of national interests.[10]

That brings us to the second myth: the Romantic myth. So firmly have Ann Radcliffe, Lord Byron, Victor Hugo, Friedrich Hölderlin, and hundreds of other European poets, painters, and writers have so thoroughly accustomed us to the phrase "Romantic Rhine" that visitors automatically use terms like "sublime" and "picturesque" to describe its vine-clad hillsides. Few other rivers in the world can match the Rhine in the number of nature icons and historic sites on its banks: Drachenfels, the Lorelei, the Mouse Tower, the Pfalz, Bacharach, Kembs, to name but a few. Fewer still can match the number of poems, songs, paintings, and other artistic productions composed in its name. In the heated political atmosphere of the 1840s, amidst intense French and German verbal sparring over who "possessed" the river, German patriots managed to pen nearly four hundred Rhine songs in the span of ten years—a dubious feat, to be sure, but one that reveals how linked the Romantic and national myths really were.[11]

Yet the river we visit today is not the same riparian habitat that the Romantics immortalized in paint and verse two hundred years ago. The river they described offers a useful snapshot of the pre-modern Rhine, the river that existed before the Rhine Navigation Commission. Their descriptions are no more useful today as a Rhine guide than an old map of Strasbourg would be to a modern-day tourist: some features would be recognizable, but most would not. The Rhine the Romantics knew possessed sinewy curves, oxbows, braids, and thousands of islands. It had a quirky unpredictable flow, and underwater cliffs so dangerous that it spawned a legend of a siren. It had sleepy fishing villages and oak-elm meadowlands on its banks. It was the site of one of Europe's most spectacular salmon runs—at the Laufenburg rapids in the Swiss Alps. It contained an overabundance of allis shad (a herring-like species known colloquially as mayfish) and a modest number of sturgeon. It also supported vibrant populations of beaver, otter, bats, and birds. That Rhine, however, is alive today only in old paintings and maps on museum walls and in the collective memory of poetry and song.

To understand how the Rhine's modern profile came into being, one must turn not to the works of the Romantics but to the blueprints of the hydraulic engineers, to the group of river specialists whom Denis Cosgrove has aptly called the "midwife to the Enlightenment and Republican vision of a new age of reason in which applied science would master the environment."[12] For even as the Romantics were praising the organic and natural aspects of the Rhine—its melancholic twists and turns, its haunting reefs and cliffs—hydraulic engineers were busy at work cutting through its curves, removing its islands, blasting out its underwater hazards, and otherwise harnessing its forces so that it would function optimally for navigation and industrial production. Its width, which once fluctuated wildly (sometimes becoming as wide as four kilometers) is now wholly pre-determined: 200 meters at Basel, 300 meters at Koblenz, 1,000 meters at Hoek van Holland. Its shipping lanes are now kept at prescribed minimum depths, roughly 2.5 meters deep. It has been straightened to such an extent that it is now 100 kilometers shorter than it was in Napoleon's day. It no longer freezes over as it once did in winter. Its banks are mostly lined with cement, rocks, and wing dams instead of woodlands. River engineers, in other words, have turned the Rhine into a mechanical and artificial stream, a shipping canal, an industrial faucet—into the very opposite of a Romantic stream!

Martin Heidegger captured this transformation best in his neo-Romantic essay "The Question Concerning Technology," published in 1949:[13]

The hydroelectric plant is set into the current of the Rhine. It sets the Rhine to supplying its hydraulic pressure which then sets the turbines turning. This turning sets those machines in motion whose thrust sets going the electric current for which the long-distance power station and its network of cables are set up to dispatch electricity. In the context of the interlocking processes pertaining to the orderly disposition of electrical energy, even the Rhine itself appears as something at our command. The hydroelectric plant is not built into the Rhine River as was the old wooden bridge that joined bank with bank for hundreds of years. Rather the river is dammed up into the power plant. What the river is now, namely, a water power supplier, derives from out of the essence of the power station. In order that we may even remotely consider the monstrousness that reigns here, let us ponder for a moment the contrast that speaks out of the two titles, "The Rhine" as dammed up into the power works, and "The Rhine" as uttered out of the art work, in Hölderlin's hymn by that name. But, it will be replied, the Rhine is still a river in the landscape, is it not? Perhaps. But how? In no other way than as an object on call for inspection by a tour group ordered there by the vacation industry.

Hölderlin's poem, it might be remembered, envisaged the "freeborn Rhine" as the fluvial incarnation of the natural man, asking rhetorically:

But where is the man
Who can remain free
His whole life long, alone
Doing his heart's desire,
Like the Rhine, so fortunate
To have been born from
Propitious heights and sacred womb?[14]

Today's Rhine is anything but free: it is harnessed from its headwaters to its delta by a chain of hydrodams, locks, reinforced banks, wing dams, reservoirs, and harbors. The person most identified with transforming the Rhine into a canal is Johann Gottfried Tulla (1770-1828), the Baden engineer who prepared the first blueprints for eliminating the oxbows, braids, and islands between Basel and Bingen. The Tulla Project got under way in 1817, just two years after the Vienna Congress had established the Rhine Navigation Commission, and it was completed sixty years later. At the time it was the largest river rectification project ever undertaken in Europe, and it made him so famous that a commemorative stone was later placed on the Rhine near Karlsruhe that reads: "Johann Gottfried Tulla: The Tamer of the Wild Rhine."[15]

Initially, the rectification work focused on land reclamation and flood control at the base of the Alps, where the river meandered wildly through the Rift valley. But by the end of the nineteenth century every kilometer of the river, from Switzerland to the Netherlands, had been rectified to one degree or another, with navigational needs increasingly taking precedence over flood control. And despite his "heroic" stature, Tulla was only the first among many engineers who contributed to the "taming" of the river and by no means the most influential one. Eduard Adolph Nobiling, the chief engineer on the Prussian Navigation Project (1850-1900), which focused on the stretch between Bingen and the Dutch-German border, probably did more to establish the Rhine's modern canal-like contours than anyone else. Richard La Nicca (Switzerland), Max Honsell (Germany),

René Koechlin (Alsace), Peter Caland (the Netherlands), and many others also exerted as much or more influence over the rectification work as did Tulla.

What is perhaps most striking about these hydraulic engineers, however, is the similarity of their biographies and blueprints despite the differences of nationality and time that separated them. They were all trained in a handful of technical schools with nearly identical curricula, and their blueprints hopped from river to river with scant attention paid to national or political allegiances. They belonged, in other words, to a loose fraternity of like-minded men (there were no prominent women among them) all schooled in the same intellectual tradition. They resided in different countries and worked on different river stretches, but the river they created looks remarkably uniform in appearance and purpose from its headwaters to its delta.

It is worthwhile briefly examining the common intellectual tradition that guided their work, for it largely prefigured the scale and scope of the various Rhine engineering projects. First and foremost, there was what one can call the Italian Renaissance tradition of river engineering that developed during the seventeenth century, with Benedetto Castelli and Domenico Guglielmini as the leading lights. The Italians mathematized river engineering by calculating for the first time the exact formula needed to determine the amount of water flowing in any given river, and they provided subsequent generations of engineers with a practical guide for taming and controlling rivers. That guide was based on two insights: first, stagnant waters breed diseases, such as typhoid and malaria; and second, natural channels are prone to flooding, hampering agricultural production. They had two simple solutions, which held sway in Europe until the mid-twentieth century: a straight river is always preferable to a meandering one; and a swift river is always better than a sluggish one. The whole purpose of river engineering from the Renaissance on was to channel water from its source to its mouth as quickly and efficiently as possible, in other words, to focus on basin drainage above all other concerns.[16]

Italian hydraulic practices spread throughout Western Europe, most especially France, where they became part of the "enlightened" curricula of the École Polytechnique and similar military engineering schools in the eighteenth century. The teachers there taught that river engineering should be harnessed to the state-building process—that is, that an enlightened ruler could reclaim river floodplains, harness water resources, and improve river commerce at one and the same time. Military matters tended to dominate the engineering profession, not the least because most of the graduates of these schools began their careers as bridge and fortress builders for the army. But civil engineers—those who went into the canal and bridge construction business, often after leaving military service—were equally important. Schooled as they were in the Renaissance-Enlightenment tradition of river engineering, European hydraulic specialists tended to view rivers as imperfect canals, defective by nature and therefore in need of improvement ("rectification" and "amelioration" in their own terminology). For the past two centuries, almost all of Europe's navigable rivers have been forged from the same overarching blueprint of canal construction; and the ideology behind it was almost without exception the Zeitgeist of optimism, the Enlightenment belief in the perfectibility of man and river.[17]

Tulla is a case in point. He worked for Karl Friedrich, the Grand Duke of Baden, an enlightened ruler who took his role as "first servant of the state" seriously. The Grand Duke recognized Tulla's mathematical gifts while Tulla was still a young man and sent him to Europe's finest engineering schools (including a year-long stint in Paris) at government expense in order to prepare him for a career in river rectification. After finishing his education, Tulla served as Baden's representative on the Napoleonic Magistrat du Rhin. His first Rhine blueprint—a "general operation plan for a [Rhine] defense" as he once called it—was submitted to Napoleon in 1812.[18] After the war, Baden and Tulla cooperated with the Vienna Congress and the Rhine Navigation Commission. Tulla's most famous dictum betrays his Italian-French training: "As a rule, no stream or river, the Rhine included, needs more than one channel; braids are redundant."[19] His approach (and that of his successors) goes a long way to explaining why today's Rhine has been harnessed into one main channel, why it more resembles a canal than a free-flowing stream, and why so many of its reinforced embankments have a fortress-like look.

The Vienna diplomats and the Rhine engineers did their job well. Today's Rhine is a superb example of how free-trade policies can stimulate commerce and trade while providing mutual benefit to all of the riparian states. It is hard to imagine how the river could be harnessed to commerce and trade to any greater degree than it is now. It is Europe's busiest waterway, transporting well over two hundred million metric tons of goods annually. Only the Mississippi, a considerably larger river, carries more freight each year. The Port of Rotterdam is the world's largest harbor. Duisburg-Ruhrort boasts the world's largest inland port. Over seven hundred ships cross the Dutch-German border each day, an average of one vessel every two minutes, twenty-four hours a day. Over fifty million humans live within its watershed, thirty million of whom rely on the Rhine for their daily drinking water. Some of Europe's largest iron, steel, chemical, automobile, aluminum, textile, potash, and paper firms are headquartered on the Rhine. Equally important for European industries are the hundreds of conventional power plants, as well as four nuclear ones, that utilize Rhine waters for cooling purposes.

The river is used for so many industrial and urban purposes that at any given moment as much as one-sixth of its water is flowing in pipelines outside its banks. A single drop of Alpine water might get utilized, cleaned, and returned to the river bed many times over on its journey downstream—by hydroelectric dams for energy, by steel and chemical plants for production, by power plants for cooling, by textile firms for dyeing, by farmers for irrigation, by mines for coal washing, by paper companies for bleaching, by cities for sanitation. This heavy use, however, has had taken its toll in the form of water pollution (heavy metals, potassium salts, organocompounds) and in terms of biological degradation.

Small wonder that the most frequent moniker heard today is not "Father Rhine" but "Europe's Romantic sewer."[20]

That brings us to the third and most contemporary Rhine myth: the myth of ecological restoration. This myth can be broken down into three components: first, the notion that water pollution represents the primary environmental problem facing the river today; second, the belief that the river will have returned to something akin to its original ecological condition once salmon swim in its channel again; and third, the belief that the river's lost floodplain can be restored through techno-fixes. One can see all three components of this myth at work by looking at the main projects of the International Commission for the Protection of the Rhine against Pollution (ICPR) from 1950 to 2000. The riparian states established ICPR in 1950 out of concern for the river's deteriorating water quality. Pollution abatement remained the commission's primary concern until the 1986 Sandoz chemical accident revealed how precarious life had become for many riverine organisms. In 1987, ICPR unveiled its "Salmon 2000" project, which was designed (as its name implies) to reintroduce a self-sustaining population of salmon by the new millennium. Its purpose was to publicly demonstrate that the riparian states were committed to habitat restoration. Then, in 1998, after multiple "once-in-a-century" floods struck the river in the short span of twelve years (1983, 1988, 1993, 1994), ICPR undertook yet another initiative—the "Action Plan on Flood Defence"—designed to reconstruct portions of the river's lost floodplain.

That the ICPR has managed to improve the Rhine's water quality significantly over the past thirty years cannot be doubted. European rivers are typically classified on a four-point sliding scale based on periodic saprobic analysis. Class I ("unpolluted") signifies that the water is oxygen-rich and nutrient-poor and thus favorable for all river life. Class II ("slightly polluted") means that the water is polluted but that oxygen levels are still normal and therefore supportive of most life. Class III ("moderately polluted") signifies the presence of organic pollutants, high bacteria levels, the near-disappearance of algae and higher plant life, and the spread of pollutant-resistant sponges, leeches, and ciliates. Class IV ("seriously polluted") means the water is so oxygen-starved and nutrient-rich that it supports bacteria, flagellates, and ciliates, but not fish or other higher life forms.[21]

In 1976—generally considered the peak pollution year—most of the stretch between Basel and Bonn belonged to Class II/III, while the stretch from Bonn to Rotterdam stood at III/IV. The entire navigable Rhine, in other words, had become so polluted that all natural biological conditions had been compromised to one degree or another, with the level of damage increasing as the water moved downstream. By 1991, the Basel-to-Bonn stretch had moved up from Class III to Class II, meaning that dissolved-oxygen levels were returning to normal. The downstream half from Bonn-to-Rotterdam also moved up a full step, from Class III/IV to Class II/III. During the same period, the Neckar tributary moved upward from III/IV to II/III, while the Main went from IV to II/III. The Wupper tributary, meanwhile, moved from IV to III, the Lippe from III to II/III, the Erft from IV to III/IV.[22]

Water quality has thus greatly improved since the mid-1970s. Nonetheless, the river still only receives a marginally passing mark. Heavily polluted parts of the river include the stretch between the Ruhr and the Lippe tributaries in North Rhine-Westphalia as well as the industrial-urban conglomerates around Basel, Strasbourg, Mannheim, Ludwigshafen, Frankfurt/Main, and Rotterdam—that is, everywhere that there are coal, steel, chemical, oil refining, pulp-and-paper, or related industries. The river is nowhere near as clean as it was in 1815, and it is not likely to become so anytime in the foreseeable future.

Water quality is a genuine environmental concern, and eliminating the river's pollutant load is certainly a precondition for any river rehabilitation. But it is also a highly anthropocentric way of looking at Rhine ecology, for it suggests that the river first became problematic in the post-1945 era when it could no longer sustain its dual role as a deliverer of clean water and as a conduit for industrial and urban waste. Non-human species, it is worth noting, did not have to await the results of ICPR water testing to take note of the fact that the Rhine was contaminated; it was obvious to them from the outset. Moreover, water pollution is but one of many reasons why there has been such a striking deterioration in the Rhine as a riparian habitat and a corresponding drop in its biodiversity. The rectification projects themselves—by giving the river a swifter, straighter channel with in-river dam-lock systems and with banks lined with cement and stone—had a far greater impact. Equally important has been the near-disappearance of the river's floodplain, a consequence of the land reclamation projects that almost always went hand-in-hand with rectification work.

One can see this bio-degradation by looking at the species most identified with rivers: fish. In 1880, the Rhine was home to forty-seven fish species. By 1975, that number had dropped to twenty-four. Improvements in water quality after 1975 reversed the downward spiral, and by 1986 a total of thirty-eight of the original forty-seven native species swam once again in the Rhine. When one adds the number of non-native species that have been introduced to the river, the Rhine actually has about the same number of species that it did two hundred years ago. But these heartening figures are deceptive for two reasons. First, many native fish species are highly endangered, their habitat restricted to a few patches of the river (typically the remnant bed that runs parallel to the Grand Canal d'Alsace in the Rift valley) where little or no rectification work has occurred. Second, many other species remain plentiful only because they are sustained through artificial propagation in fish hatcheries.[23]

In order to survive, any given Rhine species has to be able to tolerate polluted waters, nourish itself in a deeper and swifter current, and find suitable spawning and nursing grounds on the river's edge. Species dependent on aquatic plants, gravel, or sand for reproduction can no longer find a sufficient number of suitable sites in the new riverscape. Species that require slow-moving braids, backwaters, or deep-water pools are also endangered. The "universalists"—species that can adapt to a variety of spawning conditions—have generally been able to utilize secondary and tertiary biotopes as reproduction sites. But "specialists"—

species that require precise and stable breeding sites (such as the bitterling, which deposits its eggs in the gills of freshwater clams)—have had a much more difficult time surviving. Predatory species—such as the pike, zander, chub, burbot, wels, and perch, which nourish themselves on other fish—have fared poorly, a reflection of the fact that the total number of fish in the river has declined drastically. Finally, migratory species have fared worse than stationary ones because their life cycles subjected them to many stretches of the river and therefore to all of its ills.[24]

Most numerous in the river today, by far, are three so-called garbage fish: the roach, bleak, and common bream. Tolerant of polluted and degraded streams, they now account for nearly 74 percent of all fish swimming in the navigable Rhine between Basel and Hoek van Holland. The next six most common species today are the eel, dace, perch, chub, white bream, and gudgeon, which collectively account for another 23 percent of the river's fish. The remaining thirty-nine species—grayling, smelt, pike, mudminnow, ide, barbel, bitterling, minnow, rapfen, souffie, loach, burbot, stickelback, bullhead, flounder, among them—are now found in such small numbers that they collectively account for a mere 3 percent of the fish population. What this means is that just nine species account for about 97 percent of all fish swimming in the non-Alpine stretch of the river—hardly the kind of statistic that makes ecologists rejoice.[25]

The causes of this precipitous drop in biodiversity can be easily identified: engineers destroyed the longitudinal, lateral, and vertical pathways upon which most fish depend for their survival. Longitudinal pathways refer to the ability of fish to swim freely up and down a river's main and secondary channels. Lateral pathways refer to the connections between the main channel and the river edge, where most fish feed, spawn, and nurse. Vertical pathways refer to groundwater-riverwater interactions in gravel beds, which salmonids (trout and salmon) and other species use for reproduction.[26] Take away these pathways and fish populations will plummet.

The annual salmon catch, for instance, peaked at around two hundred thousand in 1885, then dropped below one hundred thousand in 1905. By 1935, the annual catch was below fifteen thousand and by the mid-1950s the industry disappeared entirely.[27] Water pollution and overfishing were the most commonly identified cause of the decline in salmon numbers at the time, but we now know that two other factors played a much larger role: dredging, which removed the gravel beds upon which the salmon depended for spawning, and dams, which blocked the salmon migratory routes and severed them from their nurseries. On the non-Alpine stretch of the river up to Basel, it was mostly gravel removal that gutted the salmon populations. In the Koblenz district, for instance, the annual catch dropped after dredgers eliminated the deep spots in the Rhine bed and rectified the Mosel mouth. Before that occurred, the Mosel had been a major salmon river. In the Cologne district, the catch plummeted when dredgers removed the gravel beds at the Sieg mouth and elsewhere. Like the Mosel, the Sieg had previously been a favorite salmon spawning ground. On the Alpine stretches, it was dams rather than dredging that undermined the salmon life cycle. The combined Swiss-Baden catch averaged 2,400 salmon annually between 1885 and 1910, then fell precipitously thereafter. The downturn coincided almost exactly with the completion of hydroelectric dams at Augst-Wyhlen (1912) and Laufenburg (1914), which severed home-bound salmon from their Alpine spawning sites. The first lock-and-dam system on the Grand Canal d'Alsace—at Kembs (1932)—performed the coup de grâce by severing the salmon completely from their Alpine streams.[28]

When we think of rivers, we tend to think of fish and channels. But actually it is the forests, meadows, and marshes of the floodplain that gives a river its geographic "breadth," its biological diversity, and its ecological dynamism. Only fish and a handful of other aquatic organisms actually spend their entire life in the river channel itself (and they, too, are dependent on the non-aquatic environment for their survival). Most riparian organisms cling to the channel bed or bank, or dwell in the wetlands, grasslands, hills, trees, bushes, meadows, and valleys around the flowing water. Wetlands are especially important because they serve as nursery grounds for fish, aquatic birds, and other animals. Wetlands also remove excess phosphorus, nitrogen, and other pollutants from the river. The roots of trees and bushes help stabilize the banks and even out the flow of water during drought and flood conditions. Foliage provides shelter, shade, and nesting spots for birds and other animals. Thus, when a river loses its floodplain it also loses most of the living space and nurseries upon which its biodiversity depends.

Unfortunately, virtually all of the Rhine's lowland forests, meadows, and marshes have been expunged over the past two hundred years, almost entirely as a consequence of commercial and economic development on its banks. In 1815, the Rhine was enveloped in nearly 2,500 square kilometers of floodplain (even more if the Alpenrhein and Aare headwaters are included in the totals). This floodplain formed a single continuous river corridor, varying in width from a few hundred meters to fifteen kilometers and stretching over one thousand kilometers from Lake Constance to the delta mouth. By 1975, most of this land had been usurped for farms, pastures, businesses, train tracks, roads, and cities. Less than 5 percent of the original riparian habitat remains anywhere close to being intact, and only about 20 percent is still subject to periodic flooding, whether it belongs to the natural or built environment. That means that even the most successful species are living on only a fraction of the space that was once available to them. For less successful species it has meant population extinction, or a precarious existence on the edge of extinction.[29]

These remnant patches, moreover, are mere patches on an otherwise anthropomorphized landscape. The largest preserved area, Kühkopf-Knoblochsaue, is less than 2,500 hectares in size. Elsewhere on the river, the protected areas tend to be between 200 and 1,000 hectares. Because of their small size and number, these natural and near-natural spaces no longer function as a continuous river corridor. Most species thus find their migratory routes and living spaces greatly constricted. Yet it is these few remaining alluvial patches that harbor almost all of the last traces of the Rhine's old-growth forests and native vegetation. One of the most famous, the Taubergiessen (1,600 hectares), contains dense stands of oak, ash, elm, poplar, mountain maple, and linden trees as well as a multitude of willows, vines, bushes, shrubs, herbs, mosses, and reeds. The density of trees, brush, and undergrowth provides a haven for insects. Nearly 40 percent of Central Europe's butterfly species are found in Taubergiessen, as are 80 percent of its dragonfly species. At home here, too, are many species of beetles, wasps, ants, and bees as well as many plants and animals on the "Red List" of endangered species.[30] The remnant oak-elm stands of Taubergiessen and similar reserves also have among the highest bird densities in all of Central Europe. But of course that also belies the fact that there are so few nesting spots left that bird populations find themselves crowded together. Of the 125 nesting species found in Baden-Württemberg, for instance, 82 are considered endangered, most of them because only 1.3 percent of the state's territory is still suitable for nesting.[31]

More mobile than fish, birds have generally been able to adapt better to the new Rhine, though many of them are now forced to use secondary biotopes rather than their primary ones for nesting, resting, and feeding. But the simple truth is that these remnant patches are neither geographically diverse nor large enough to preserve the Rhine's original bird species. Birds that nest on gravel and sand banks—the plover, sandpiper, and common tern—have become rare or disappeared from the river. Forest destruction has reduced the habitat of woodpeckers and other birds that utilize tree holes as nests. Twenty-three bird species can no longer be found anywhere between Lake Constance and Bingen, including the night heron, black stork, and pintail duck. Another twenty-three species—the sand martin, red kite, quail, and bluethroat among them—have declined significantly in numbers. Gone from the marshlands of the Lower Rhine and delta are yet another twenty-three bird species. Endangered there are all diving birds, songbirds, and terns, as well as most herons, ducks, geese, falcons, and wading birds.[32]

Amphibians and reptiles have diminished in numbers as the floodplain has vanished, though only three—the tree frog, dice snake, and adder—are considered endangered. The tree frog has suffered from a dearth of still-water areas for its larvae and a reduction in the number of trees and foliage. Water pollution and canalized banks have driven dice snakes from their former habitat, while adder became rare when their hunting grounds were turned into farmland and pasture. Some insect species have also been adversely affected by Rhine engineering—though the exact impact is obscured by the absence of clear-cut empirical data from the past. Most ominous has been the dramatic drop in mayfly, stonefly, and caddisfly populations—all crucial to the Rhine's food chain. Dependent on clean water, their taxa numbers dropped from 111 in 1900 to 3 in 1971. It rose again as water quality improved, but as recently as 1980 there were still only 46 taxa found on the Rhine, less than half the original number.[33]

The Rhine's other invertebrate populations have also been affected by engineering and the loss of floodplain vegetation—though the record is sketchy because the first systematic investigations took place in the early twentieth century, by which time the rectification was already well under way. Lithophiles (organisms that adhere to hard surfaces)—such as freshwater limpets, snails, leeches, sponges, moss animals, and hydras—have generally prospered in the new Rhine environment, for obvious reasons. Previously confined to the Rhine's canyon walls, they now are free to move at will along the river's rock-lined artificial embankments. And many non-native species have crawled to the Rhine via canals and embankments, or hitchhiked there on the hulls of ships. The number of leech species, for instance, grew from four in 1900 to twelve in 1980. During the same time period, the number of crustacean species (crabs and shrimps) rose from three to thirteen, and the number of mollusks (clams and snails) from twenty to twenty-three. But here, too, the apparent increase in biodiversity masked a more troubling development. Several native species—including the Rhine mussel, an age-old inhabitant—disappeared entirely from the river. New species that spread successfully to the Rhine were more tolerant than the native ones of saltier, warmer, and oxygen-depleted (eutrophic) water. The non-native zebra mussel, for instance, is highly tolerant of salt and has therefore come to dominate the Rhine's bottom-dwelling (benthic) communities through sheer force of numbers. Other newcomers—the freshwater crayfish, shrimp, beach flea, and river snail, among them—are all physiologically, morphologically, and behaviorally adapted to industrial pollutants, dissolved salts, and other harsh river conditions.[34]

"More faunal changes have occurred in the past one hundred fifty years," concluded the biologist Ragnar Kinzelbach in a recent Rhine study, "than in the previous ten thousand years."[35] Modern river engineering, in other words, has had the equivalent impact of an ice age on the Rhine's biology—and in a much shorter span of time. Transformations of this dimension can not be undone by small projects such as Salmon 2000 and the lesser-known Stork Plan. Salmon 2000 has focused on reestablishing salmon populations on the few remaining tributaries that still have suitable gravel beds, chiefly the Sieg, Bröl, Lahn, Saynbach, Bruche, Ill, and Lauter. The goal has been to create a stable population of around twenty thousand mature returning salmon per year, a tiny fraction of the estimated half million that once migrated up the Rhine each year.[36] The Stork Plan, a Dutch project, has resulted in the reconstruction of alluvial forestland on the Waal (the Rhine's main delta channel) at Millinger Waard, Sint Andries, Blauwe Kamer, and Duurse Waarden. Black stork have benefited from the new living space, as have a few other birds and some mammals, notably the beaver. But the scope of this project (like Salmon 2000) was small and resulted only in the token restoration of a few "charismatic" species.[37]

The newest Rhine plan, the Action Plan on Flood Defence, got under way in 1998. It potentially holds out the best prospect for habitat restoration since it has as its stated goal the reestablishment of as much floodplain as feasible; but in practice its impact will probably be limited. On the river itself, current plans foresee a restoration of around 160 square kilometers of riverine space and the renaturalization of 1,100 kilometers of channel embankment. Within the entire basin, about 1,000 square kilometers of former floodplain will be restored and 11,000 kilometers of feeder streams renaturalized. These figures are not inconsiderable in their own right, but they are small when one remembers that the Rhine's original floodplain was once nearly 2,500 square kilometers in size, and its catchment area is 185,000 square kilometers. Only a small fraction of the Rhine's watershed can be restored easily: most of the river's floodplain has been turned over to industrial and agricultural use. Given this limitation, the riparian governments mostly plan to construct artificial polders (special water-storage areas) designed to hold back the overflow during peak periods, rather than undertake the more costly (and politically risky) effort to restore a large portion of the river's original floodplain. Unfortunately, artificial polders are a techno-fix that will do little to re-establish the river's natural dynamics or significantly augment the amount of river-edge habitat available to non-human species.[38]

Conclusion

When the Vienna diplomats began regulating Rhine affairs nearly two hundred years ago, they placed the river under a specific kind of international regime. They encharged the Rhine Navigation Commission with the task of improving shipping and navigation and nothing else. By doing so, they unwittingly created an ecological vacuum: all of the riparian states had an interest in maximizing their share of the Rhine's commerce and trade, while none felt any individual responsibility for preserving the river as a riparian habitat. All benefited from the commercial development, yet none had any sense of custodianship. By the time they finally got around to creating ICPR in 1950, "Father Rhine" was already languishing in its artificial bed. Put in more modern terminology, the Vienna Congress thought globally and acted globally. The riparian cities and states displayed remarkably little sense of local, regional, or even *national* guardianship— despite all the Franco-German rhetoric of possession and ownership.

Hydraulic engineers exacerbated the situation because they viewed rivers as mere sluiceways for transporting water rather than as complex biological habitats. They envisaged a river in a mechanical (that is, "enlightened") way, treating it as a physio-chemical entity; and they manipulated its channel in a linear way, as if it could be separated from its floodplain. They failed to grasp what every Romantic instinctively knew: that a river, as a carrier of water, lies at the confluence of the biological and physio-chemical worlds, that it is, in Richard White's apt phrase, an "organic machine."[39] By failing to see a river first and foremost as a riparian habitat, they set in motion an ecological revolution on the Rhine, the effects of which would not be felt until a century later as fish populations began to dwindle and as species went extinct.

The Rhine of 1815 cannot be restored, at least not without undoing much of the rectification work upon which fifty million people now depend, slogan-like programs such as "Salmon 2000" and the "Flood Defence" notwithstanding. Improvements in water quality have already done much to improve conditions on the Rhine. But if European states really intend to revive the river, they will have to pay far more attention to re-establishing the river's former woodlands and wetlands in order to maximize the diversity of habitat. That will require a longterm political commitment on the part of the riparian states and considerable ingenuity on the part of contemporary hydraulic engineers. The engineering work of the past is now deeply embedded in today's Rhine in the form of a straightened channel and reinforced banks. Undoing the river's damage without undoing the river's ability to transport goods will not be easy.

Notes

1. Marc Bloch, "Le Rhin," in *Annales d'histoire économique et sociale* 5 (1933): 84.
2. For an overview of Rhine history, see Horst-Johs Tümmers, *Rheinromantik. Romantik und Reisen am Rhein* (Cologne, 1968); Horst Johannes Tümmers, *Der Rhein. Ein europäischer Fluß und seine Geschichte* (Munich, 1994); and Mark Cioc, *The Rhine: An Eco-Biography, 1815–2000* (Seattle, 2002).
3. Julius Caesar, *The Gallic War*, The Loeb Classical Library (Cambridge, Mass., 1963), Book IV, 10 (191).
4. Unless otherwise indicated, all facts and figures about the Rhine come from the International Commission for the Hydrology of the Rhine Basin (CHR), *Der Rhein unter der Einwirkung des Menschen—Ausbau, Schiffahrt, Wasserwirtschaft* (Lelystad, 1993).
5. Cited by Hans Boldt, "Deutschlands hochschlagende Pulsader," in *Der Rhein. Mythos und Realität eines europäischen Stromes*, edited by Hans Boldt (Cologne, 1988), 30.
6. Ibid., 31.
7. The documents relating to the Vienna Congress and the establishment of the Rhine Navigation Commission have been collected in *Rheinurkunden. Sammlung zwischenstaatlicher Vereinbarungen, landesrechtlicher Ausführungsverordnungen und sonstiger wichtiger Urkunden über die Rheinschiffahrt seit 1803*, 2 vols. (Munich, 1918).
8. Cited in Pierre Ayçoberry and Marc Ferro, *Une histoire du Rhin* (Pari, 1981), 370–71.
9. Article 5 of the Paris Peace Treaty (1814), as cited in *Rheinurkunden*, vol. 1, 36.
10. Brief historical sketches of the Rhine Navigation Commission can be found in J. P. Chamberlain, *The Regime of the International Rivers: Danube and Rhine*, Ph. D. Diss. (Columbia University, 1923); Edwin J. Clapp, *The Navigable Rhine* (Boston, 1911); Dethard Freiherr von dem Bussche-Haddenhausen, "Einiges über die Geschichte und Tätigkeit der Zentralkommission für die Rheinschaffahrt," *Beiträge zur Rheinkunde* (1968): 13–29.
11. See Cecelia Hopkins Porter, *The Rhine as Musical Metaphor: Cultural Identity in German Romantic Music* (Boston, 1996), especially 38–47.
12. Denis Cosgrove, "An Elemental Division: Water Control and Engineered Landscape," in *Water, Engineering and Landscape: Water Control and Landscape Transformation in the Modern Period*, eds. Denis Cosgrove and Geoff Petts (London: 1990), 6.
13. Martin Heidegger, *The Question Concerning Technology and Other Essays*, translated by William Lovitt (New York, 1977), 16.

14. Friedrich Hölderlin, *Hymns and Fragments*, translated by Richard Sieburth (Princeton, 1984), 71.

15. For a succinct biography, see Martin Eckoldt, "Johann Gottfried Tulla—Zu seinem 200. Geburtstag," *Beiträge zur Rheinkunde*, no. 22 (1970): 19–22.

16. See especially Cesare S. Maffioli, *Out of Galileo: The Science of Waters 1628–1718* (Rotterdam, 1994); Norman Smith, *Man and Water: A History of Hydro-Technology* (London, 1975).

17. André E. Guillerme, *The Age of Water: The Urban Environment in the North of France, A.D. 300–1800* (College Station, Texas, 1983), 196–209.

18. Cited by Traude Löbert, *Die Oberrheinkorrektion in Baden. Zur Umweltgeschichte des 19. Jahrhunderts*, Mitteilungen des Institutes für Wasserbau und Kulturtechnik der Universität Karlsruhe (Karlsruhe, 1997), 98.

19. Cited by Max Honsell, *Die Korrektion des Oberrheins von der Schweizer Grenze unterhalb Basel bis zur Großherzogthum Hessischen Grenze unterhalb Mannheim* (Karlsruhe, 1885), 5.

20. For succinct summaries of Rhine environmental problems, see Günther Reichelt, *Laßt den Rhein leben!* (Düsseldorf, 1986); and Christoph Bernhardt, "Zeitgenössische Kontroversen über die Umweltfolgen der Oberrheinkorrektion im 19. Jahrhundert," in *Zeitschrift für die Geschichte des Oberrheins* (1998): 293–319.

21. Reichelt, *Laßt den Rhein leben!* 85–7.

22. Deutsche Kommission zur Reinhaltung des Rheins, *Rheinbericht 1990* (Düsseldorf, 1991), 19–22.

23. Anton Lelek and Günter Buhse, *Fische des Rheins—früher und heute* (Berlin, 1992), 34–5 and 186.

24. Ibid., 30–2 and 43–4.

25. Ibid., 37–8.

26. Ian G. Cowx and Robin L. Welcomme, eds., *Rehabilitation of Rivers for Fish. A Study Undertaken by the European Inland Fisheries Advisory Commission of FAO* (Oxford, 1998), 12–19.

27. Statistics from Barbara Froehlich-Schmitt, *Salmon 2000* (Koblenz, 1994), 6.

28. On the fate of the salmon, see W. Fehlmann, *Die Ursachen des Rückganges der Lachsfischerei im Hochrhein*, Beilage zum Jahresbericht der Kantonsschule Schaffhausen (Schaffhausen, 1926); Walter Jens and Ragnar Kinzelbach, "Der Lachs," *Mainzer Naturwissenschaftliches Archiv*, no. 13 (1990): 57–63.

29. Hartmut and Antje Solmsdorf, "Schutzwürdigen Bereiche im Rheintal," *Beiträge zur Rheinkunde* 27 (1975): 28–32.

30. Bruno Kremer, "Die Auengebiete des südlichen Oberrheins—Chance für die Natur oder verschwindende Naturlandschaft?" *Beiträge zur Rheinkunde* 41 (1989): 56–67.

31. Thomas Tittizer and Falk Krebs, eds., *Ökosystemforschung: Der Rhein und seine Auen. Eine Bilanz* (Berlin, 1996), 198–204.

32. Ibid., 198–204.

33. Ibid., 194–7.

34. Ibid., 247–56 and 305–6.

35. Ragnar Kinzelbach, ed., *Die Tierwelt des Rheins einst und jetzt: Symposium zum Jubiläum der Rheinischen Naturforschenden Gesellschaft und des Naturhistorischen Museums Mainz am 9. November 1984* (Mainz, 1985), 40.

36. The plan is laid out in detail in International Commission for the Protection of the Rhine (ICPR), *Ist der Rhein wieder ein Fluss für Lachse? – "Lachs 2000"* (Koblenz, 1999), 4–39.

37. For a comprehensive overview of the Stork Plan, see Dick de Bruin, et al., *Ooievaar. De toekomst van het rivierengebied* (Arnhem, 1987), 9–20.

38. International Commission for the Protection of the Rhine (ICPR), *Action Plan on Flood Defence* (Koblenz, 1998), 8–15.

39. Richard White, *The Organic Machine: The Remaking of the Columbia River* (New York, 1995).

Chapter 3

LANDSCAPE AS HISTORY
Pückler-Muskau, The "Green Prince" of Germany

Linda Parshall

Upon the death of his father in 1811, the twenty-five-year old Count Hermann Ludwig Heinrich von Pückler-Muskau (1785-1871) inherited several pieces of property, by far the largest of which, the *Standesherrschaft* of Muskau, extended about nine square miles on either side of the Neisse River. Over the next three decades the Count, later Prince, was to turn this estate into a vast park in the English landscape manner.[1] Subsequently he undertook a similar transformation at Branitz, a smaller family estate only twenty-five miles distant. It was never his intention, however, to slavishly imitate the English style but rather to develop a particular, regional style, a German landscape that would reflect and embody his own ideas about family, history, and society. His parks would stand as enduring monuments to his own personal achievements as a member of the German aristocracy. Pückler's vision took shape in the first two decades of the nineteenth century, when Germany itself was seeking to define itself as a nation, first culturally and then politically. Romantic conceptions of nature and enlightened social ideals informed Pückler's own aspirations as a landscape designer, writer, and extravagant, if chronically insolvent, landowner of liberal tendencies.

A strikingly melodramatic episode offers some insight into Pückler's sense of destiny in assuming the role of landed aristocrat. In 1815, four years after his father's death, he orchestrated—and recorded for posterity—a scene that might have come straight out of an E.T.A. Hoffmann tale and, indeed, may have inspired one.[2] The hour is midnight, the place a church and graveyard. Accompanied by a sexton, the way lit by torches, the count approaches the church and, once inside, dismisses his escort and descends alone into the crypt. There he con-

Notes for this section begin on page 68.

fronts an array of entombed ancestors, most directly those in the three coffins that already lie open at his request. Alongside Pückler's grandfather are two figures from the family's more ancient history: a colonel who fought in the Thirty Years' War and the "beautiful Ursula" (known locally as "evil Ursula"), both proudly traced back to Rüdiger of *Nibelungenlied* fame.[3] Although at Pückler's touch Ursula's silk mantel dissolves into worm-ridden dust, this does not deter him from lingering in contemplation of his inheritance and its burdens, his responsibilities, and his hopes. This eerie scene and its recording reflect Pückler's infamous flair for theatricality, his braggadocio, his "gothic" sensibility, and his gift for self-promotion.

Pückler's preoccupation with questions of self-definition, with the effectiveness of his actions, indeed with issues of fate versus individual will, was not unusual for his time. And by the early nineteenth century the world of nature, often the garden itself, had become the symbolic arena in which the debate over history and human purpose was pursued. This was Pückler's choice as main stage. We find gardens, real and imagined, figuring importantly elsewhere in Germany too. In Goethe's *Die Wahlverwandtschaften* (*Elective Affinities*), a landscape park is a major protagonist, a setting so convincingly evoked that maps have been drawn of it.[4] Though fictional, this garden has a history, a present, and—through the reader—a future. The novel's characters work to transform an estate into a landscape garden, an endeavor which transforms them in return: nature is not merely a picturesque backdrop but woven into their lives and fate. For Walter Benjamin, it is nature as the tellurian, the earth-related, influence that drives the whole plot of this complex novel.[5] In compelling ways, the same could be said of Pückler and his estates at Muskau and Branitz, for in making them into English-style landscapes not unlike the *Wahlverwandtschaften* park, his own destiny became interwoven with the natural setting and transformed along with it. As Goethe did in his novel, Pückler used the designed landscape on multiple levels in his writings and in determining the course of his life, exploiting it as an arena for representing aesthetic and social ideas but also developing it as a place, a space to be explored, a work of art that is only complete when realized by a visitor, but that as an aesthetic experience can never be fixed. As something that was both nature and art, the garden was appealingly paradoxical, mercurial, and accordingly potent.

The sources for Pückler's aspirations can best be found in the late eighteenth century. Goethe himself designed parks in the 1770s (the Park an der Ilm in Weimar, for example) and imaginary ones in the early 1800s (*Elective Affinities* was published in 1809).[6] But more importantly, the ground for Pückler's thinking was laid by English theorists and their principle Continental interpreter C.C.L. Hirschfeld, the German writer on landscape design who published a five-volume *Theorie der Gartenkunst* (*Theory of Garden Art*) in the years 1779-85.[7] Hirschfeld urged the German-speaking lands to perfect their own gardens. He saw the new, natural style developed especially in England not just as the ideal way to assist nature in expressing her inherent power—the proper goal of the new garden, he maintained—but also as an inspirational focus for the nurturing of a national consciousness and cultural unity among his countrymen. In a chapter on "Gardens in Germany," Hirschfeld ridicules the slavish imitation of the symmetrical "French" manner and calls upon Germany to turn to the "resources of its own spirit" and to "design gardens that bear the stamp of German ingenuity." He asks, "Is it not possible to envision and then realize a style that is German enough to deserve the name?"[8] His answer—suggested throughout the *Theory*— lies in his claim for a German affinity with the natural world. He praises the varied and manifest beauties of the German landscape and offers a warning against aping foreign styles and overburdening a scene with too much of the "picturesque." Pückler followed Hirschfeld's guidance in these regards and also heeded him in the moderate use of nationalistic references, such as introducing elements that would invoke feelings of patriotism or displaying garden inscriptions in the vernacular.[9] However, Pückler's approach was less literal than Hirschfeld's, more metaphorical, and finally more subjective. He interpreted Hirschfeld as calling not for a revolution in the art of gardening but for a return to nature herself. And here perhaps most important was the belief in the aesthetic and moral power of nature's own loveliness, to which mankind could add by artful arrangement, by carefully chosen vistas, by guiding a visitor to experience the unfolding, participatory delights of a garden visit. The English themselves touted the political implications of their natural landscape style, and these same values of liberty and openness were inherent in Hirschfeld's call for a "national garden" that would embody the "spirit of the nation" (*Geist der Nation*). He endorsed the English insistence that the style was democratic, the opposite of the despotism of the formal garden, and Pückler, like Hirschfeld, felt that the republican ideals of equality and fairness displayed by such a garden could be achieved under the enlightened paternalism of a sovereign prince. Here again, nature was the model, for in the untouched landscape all and sundry could experience her beauty and truth, all could be moved both sensually and ethically. As one of Pückler's contemporaries commented, "Nature is republican,"[10] and for many popular philosophers a properly designed landscape garden could equal and sometimes surpass nature's raw power as a force for good.

The new approach to landscape was thus political in a philosophically detached way; many enlightened intellectuals agreed that Germany, like its gardens, could be brought *naturally* to a state of freedom and equality. There was no need for violence against the existing ruling structure; given no centralized power to revolt against, there was no need to follow the French.[11] Beginning around 1800, the Romantic movement added support to this view along with an enhanced appreciation for the past—a love of ruins, an idealized notion of the Middle Ages, the Germanic ethos, attention to the transitoriness of the seasons. This taste was matched in the informal garden. The Romantics also developed enlightened ideas about the state and the individual that led to a questioning of absolutism in politics and in aesthetics and to a championing of individuality, emotion, and freedom of spirit. Pückler's romantic subjectivity and political idealism fed on these new declarations of freedom in defining his own purpose and that of his landscape parks.

Early Directions

Born the first son of a noble family of Sachsen-Anhalt, Pückler quickly showed a propensity to misbehave that continued throughout his life. At fifteen, he went off to study at the University of Leipzig, where he adopted a lifestyle that occasioned broken hearts, tasty gossip, and many duels.[12] After three years, he abandoned the university to pursue a military career, and there he excelled, rising quickly to the rank of general. He soon changed direction and in 1806 headed south on the first of his many travels rather than fight on the side of Napoleon against Prussia—something he would have been bound to do, since his ancestral lands lay in the electorate of Saxony which had declared for the French side.

When he returned to Muskau in 1810, his mind was already consumed with a passion for transforming the landscape and releasing its hidden beauty. Pückler's wit and ingenuity allowed him to pursue that dream for decades, although his plans were repeatedly interrupted. The initial hiatus came when he departed Muskau to fight in the wars after all, not for but against Napoleon, serving first alongside the Russians, then joining the Duke of Sachsen-Weimar and later (1813-14) the Prussians.[13] After the truce, he made his first trip to England in the retinue of the Russian emperor and the Prussian king. This was crucial to his later designs upon the land, for he returned to Muskau in 1815 inspired by English ideals of public life and social structure as well as by the informal style of

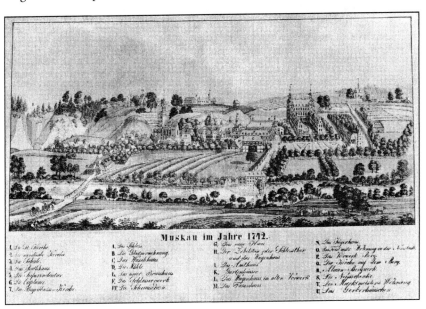

Figure 1. View of village of Muskau in 1742.

the English landscape parks. It was at this point that he enacted the midnight visit to his family crypt. The particulars of his vision were not yet fixed, but his ambition and self-confidence were unbounded. To achieve his ideals, Pückler would change the course of rivers, drain marshes, raise hills, transport hundreds of thousands of trees (some enormous), and move vast numbers of huge stones (including the entire fortifications of a palace). None of this daunted him then or later.

Pückler's ancestral lands presented a challenge that was political as well as aesthetic. Muskau lay in the region known as Lusatia, or Lausitz, some one hundred miles southeast of Berlin—about three days travel in his time.[14] Lying west of the Oder and north of the Czech border, the area was inhabited by both German- and Wendish- (or Sorbian-) speaking people. In fact, at the time of Pückler's birth, thirteen of the more than forty villages on the family estate were Wendish, and there was a Wendish church, school, and cemetery, though the largest town—that of Muskau itself, which adjoined the family palace—was solidly German. An early print [Fig. 1] shows the town of Muskau and its proximity to the palace at the upper right, with the Neisse River at the bottom. Pückler's estate extended far beyond this view, stretching across the sandy flatlands and low hills on both sides of the river; there was little variation and interesting vistas were scarce. As a contemporary admirer of Pückler's skills put it: "Nature was but an ungenerous step-mother to Muskau; she provided nothing for the lay-out of a park—no cliffs or waterfalls, no woodlands, no meadows, no mountains and valleys; nothing but pine and native grasses grows on the flat sandy ground. In rare spots, the Neisse has cut itself a deeper passage through the soil so that a few dales have been formed."[15] Pückler had inherited a huge canvas on which to paint his ambitious picture—a metaphor he himself was fond of—and if he saw nature as a rather too modest assistant at times, he managed to transform his property into a model for his countrymen, a locus for German ideals of landscape.

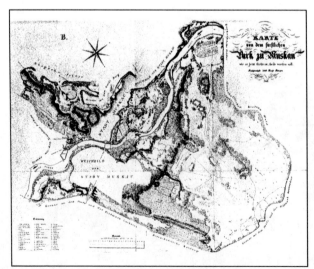

Figure 2. A map of the park, "as it is and is to become," from the *Andeutungen* (end piece). Photo courtesy of the Dumbarton Oaks Research Library and Collections, Washington, DC.

Figure 3. Muskau – view from the Gloriette (*Andeutungen*, plate 18). Photo courtesy of the Dumbarton Oaks Research Library and Collections, Washington, DC.

When Pückler assumed his title in 1811, the property was already very large. It also came burdened with a huge debt to which he was destined to add. Although the land was not particularly fertile, it supported over eight thousand people and a number of industries. Fruit trees, wheat, and other grains were cultivated, and there was even an attempt at raising tobacco. Still today, Muskau Park ranks among the great landscaping achievements of its era, although many of its structures are in ruins and the estate is severed by a political border. Forty percent of its now much-reduced acreage lies in Germany, the remainder in Poland.[16] A map of the park as Pückler planned to develop it [Fig. 2] shows the palace and several villages on lands bisected by the Neisse River.[17] Another view [Fig. 3] gives an impression of the landscape. In fact, over half of the land was timbered and managed through an early and carefully controlled method of clear-cutting whereby the forests were divided and sub-divided allowing restricted harvesting and a turnover rate of one hundred forty years. Bee-keeping flourished. One entrepreneur on Pückler's property had over eight thousand hives resulting in good local honey and a flourishing candle-making industry.[18] There were fisheries on the 153 ponds and 16 lakes. A number of mines yielded granite, porphyry, flint, iron pyrites, and alum. Varied and abundant game inhabited the forests, over thirteen thousand sheep grazed on the meadows, and a local brewery won praise for a particularly tasty Weizenbier. A liberal, enlightened landowner and overlord, the young Pückler was reportedly respected and liked by his subjects and tenants. His father had been a benevolent overlord, a tradition that Pückler continued; everyone, vassals and freemen, could turn to an independent court to settle disputes; guilds were sanctioned, streets were kept mostly repaired, and the numerous schools were supported by an annual taxation of all subjects, whether or not they had children.

Pückler aspired to bring his people happiness and prosperity, and once he became convinced that this would come from the creation and maintenance of a park, he threw himself into the project with zeal. He quickly invited his Berlin friend Friedrich Schinkel to visit Muskau, and the two traversed the grounds together discussing possible architectural embellishments, many of which Schinkel sketched. For the landscape design, he turned to the broad sweeping vistas of English models such as those by Lancelot "Capability" Brown, whom Pückler dubbed the "Shakespeare of gardening."[19] For landscape theory, and for confirmation of the profound importance of his undertaking, he could turn to Hirschfeld: "In a certain respect the art of gardening can justifiably claim advantage over the other fine arts. It is art, yet woven into nature more than any of its sister arts."[20]

Pückler observed that parks in the British Isles managed to augment but never obviously control nature, so that each footpath seemed to wander in total harmony with the ground, each vista opened randomly yet at a point of utmost surprise or loveliness, each tree or group of trees was perfectly situated to proclaim its own beauty while setting off the surrounding meadow. He records his astonishment at Blenheim, which Brown had landscaped in the 1760s, its scale, its natural, flourishing plantings, the deceptively untouched majesty of its plummeting cascades.[21] In Ireland, he finds perfect harmony between art and nature at Kenmare, where no bush seems planted by design, no vista or path can be imagined otherwise. Here, too, all views are created with great care for the effect on the visitor; the beauties of the site are never laid totally bare but always veiled enough to allow the imagination room to play: "For a perfect park,—in other words, a tract of country idealized *by art*—should be like a good book, which suggests *at least* as many new thoughts and feelings as it expresses."[22] Such passages reflect Pückler's familiarity with Hirschfeld's insistence on the interactive roles of art and nature in creating a perfect garden. In designing his own landscaped park at Muskau, Pückler was to follow similar principles, thus fulfilling Hirschfeld's two basic tenets of garden art: to shape the elements of nature so as to increase their effect on the garden visitor and to intermingle appropriate artistic elements in order to heighten this impression. As Hirschfeld explains: "A garden can move the imagination and senses powerfully, more powerfully than can an area whose beauty comes from nature alone. Call, therefore, upon the natural beauty of the landscape; but call upon art as well, so that its influence can increase this beauty even more."[23]

Such convictions led Pückler to broaden the scope of his visionary plans for Muskau. He recognized that before he could transform his estate into an ideal park, he would need to expand his holdings to ensure that all important vistas be guaranteed and appear natural. Since some desirable property was not yet in his possession, he posted a proclamation on the *Rathaus* door in the town of Muskau. Here are the first two sentences:

Since I have now decided to make Muskau my permanent residence for the remainder of my life, in order personally to watch over the welfare of my good citizens and subjects with paternal care and preferring to let them, rather than strangers, benefit from my income, I do not doubt that every inhabitant of this city will, after serious thought, be happy to grant me the chance to fulfill one of my strongest inclinations, the execution of which will not only bring each and every one of them pleasure but which already now and even more in the future can only redound to their true advantage. I mean the laying-out of a park.[24]

Sentiments of enlightened absolutism are apparent here, as is the thirty-year-old Pückler's caring, paternal attitude towards his subjects and his view of this park as an investment in their future. He goes on to explain his wish to acquire certain pieces of land, including a village street, and promises to set up a panel to negotiate the transactions (two representatives chosen by the people, two by him); he will pay with money, land, or both; disputes will be settled by yet another independent body, and so forth. This is certainly a more democratic attitude than the wholesale removal of villages that Oliver Goldsmith decries in "The Deserted Village" of 1770.[25] Pückler vows in return to give people work on his estate and to build, within six years, a new *Rathaus*, a city gate, and some other structures. He further promises—or better said, threatens—that should the sales not be completed within one year, he will pack up and leave Muskau—along with all his belongings, retinue, and even what he can take of the palace itself.

The conditions of his proclamation were met, and he acquired all the property he wanted, although at a steep price (some have claimed he paid six times the value). But Pückler, who always tried to live as though money were no obstacle, not only bought the land but immediately set about pouring vast sums into shaping and maintaining it; by employing over two hundred people for the next three decades, he helped the district survive catastrophic crop failures and other calamities.

In 1817, shortly after his successful property acquisitions, Pückler made a further commitment to his Muskau estate by marrying Lucie von Pappenheim, the daughter of Karl August Hardenberg, Chancellor of Prussia. She quickly became devoted to Pückler's plans for the park. However, after just six years during which the couple expended all of his money and her substantial fortune as well, their plans were only partially realized. In order to salvage their dream, they decided to divorce, freeing Pückler to marry a rich heiress. This plan did not imply a permanent separation; neither of them intended ever to abandon their land. On the contrary, while Pückler was gone on a nearly three-year fortune hunt through the British Isles, Lucie stayed behind, oversaw the continuing work on the park and collected Pückler's long, genial, and near-daily epistles addressed to his *Schnucke* ("lambkins"), *vielgeliebtes Schnucktier* ("little lamby-poo"), and other such pet names.[26] Judging from his letters, it appears that he was seeking out landscape garden models even more avidly than he was eyeing young women as potential secondary mistresses of Muskau.[27] How a young bride would have reacted to this triangulation we can only surmise, for after two or three near successes Pückler finally returned home without an heiress. Thereupon the notion of editing a selection of his many letters was concocted, resulting in one of the literary triumphs of the era, a multi-volume chronicle of his 1826-29 journey published anonymously as the *Briefe eines Verstorbenen* ("Letters of a Deceased Man").[28]

Theory and Practice; Words and Deeds

The *Briefe*, the most popular and substantial of Pückler's travel books, testify to the multifariousness of his engagement with the world. Even expurgated as they were, and ascribed to an anonymous, fictively dead author, these volumes were a great hit: insightful, gossipy, witty, critical yet admiring … and often racy and downright outrageous. It has been said that the *Briefe* may well have caused a bigger stir than Byron's *Childe Harold*.[29] Certainly both Pückler and Byron—whom Pückler admired very much—would have loved Oscar Wilde's observation: "I never travel without my diary. One should always have something sensational to read in the train." Then, as now, all publicity was good publicity, and Pückler's behavior was typically designed to draw attention, for example his custom of riding around Berlin in a carriage pulled by four large-horned stags. He knew how to titillate in his writings, too. His later book about Egypt contains passages printed upside-down and clearly marked "not for ladies"—ensuring that no-one would skip them.[30]

Pückler's long life (he lived to be eighty-six) and his extraordinary energy and romantic enthusiasms, his ironic wit and insight into his own and his society's singularities, left a wide-ranging record of accomplishments. Although the *Briefe* were his most famous literary contribution, he produced a number of other popular works. There were accounts of his many later travels, for he abandoned the landscape of his native region to visit not only the expected spots on the Continent and the British Isles, but also Greece, Anatolia, Egypt, Nubia, and the Sudan, publishing his impressions upon his return.[31] In all of these books, his interest in landscape and gardens persists as a leitmotif. Of particular significance, however, are his descriptions of British parks and gardens in the *Briefe* (he is said to have visited nearly every important site) and his influential book of 1834, *Andeutungen über Landschaftsgärtnerei* ("Hints on Landscape Gardening"), which expounds his theories on garden design, describes their application at Muskau, and ends with detailed descriptions of three different walking tours through the property—the theory, practice, and experience of garden art.[32] This publication, along with his unrestrained enthusiasm for nature, earned him the epithet *der grüne Fürst* (the Green Prince). Some of Pückler's contemporaries found other epithets for him as well: "the Goethe of landscape gardening," or, less flatteringly, "Parkomaniac" or "Count Schmorltork" (from Dickens *Pickwick Papers*)—these latter from those who judged his preoccupations to be more like obsessions, his wit and charm to be overworked. His copious letters and travel writings put him much in step with the times, for the reading public was expanding remarkably. The Grand Tour was everyone's goal—at least via an armchair.[33] In his own day, Pückler's work was well known, and his reputation spread through Germany and Europe and to America as well, where he was seen as a prophet of city planning and inspired a number of important landscape designers such as Charles Eliot, Samuel Parsons, and Henry Vincent Hubbard.[34]

Pückler made extraordinary contributions to the philosophy of landscape design in deed as well as word, initially and most grandly at Muskau as well as at Babelsberg in Potsdam and Schloß Tiefurt in Weimar. When financial woes at last forced him and Lucie to sell Muskau and retreat to Branitz in 1846, Pückler was initially downhearted and disillusioned. But he managed to rally his spirits, and before his death in 1875 he created a landscape there that essentially reflects the ideas he applied at Muskau. Furthermore, many of his plans for Muskau Park itself were carried out even after his departure and for some time after his death by Eduard Petzold, a gardener who originally apprenticed under Pückler at Muskau and whom the new owners engaged to continue the dream.[35]

Self-Fashioning

Pückler's writings and his gardens were acts of self-presentation. Both are personal creations of symbolic space; both interpret and disguise his life; both contribute to his legacy. His major landscape designs were semblances of a world meant to nurture his own family and dependants and to define a way of life, to capture a history. They are both representational and experiential, visual and tactile, multi-dimensional, synaesthetic, and meant to be read both synchronically and diachronically.

For his sense of self and his legacy, he again found inspiration on his journey to England, where he managed to socialize with the leaders of genteel society, who offered him entrée into their homes and country estates (and who later devoured the English translation of his letters with remarkable enthusiasm, despite—or perhaps because of—the occasionally mocking, gossipy tone).[36] A visit to Warwick Castle was particularly affecting, his ebullient report to Lucie being remarkable for its lyrical descriptions and for its personal reflections on the owner and his heritage. The letter is headed "Warwick, December 28th, 1826," indicating that this was one of Pückler's early garden experiences in England. While the beauty of the grounds fills him with astonishment—it was for him a *"Zauberwort"*[37]—the historical and political importance of the owner and his ancestry clearly resounds with Pückler's own personal ambitions. It is worth quoting from this letter at some length, since it not only displays Pückler's literary talent but also reveals, I believe, an important model for his visionary landscape plans as well as for his own self-fashioning.

> The Earls of Warwick were once the mightiest vassals of England ... the great Beauchamp,[39] Earl of Warwick, boasted of having deposed three kings, and placed as many on the vacant throne. This was his castle, standing ever since the ninth century, and in the possession of the same family since the reign of Elizabeth. A tower of the castle, said to have been built by Beauchamp himself, remains unaltered; and the whole stands colossal and mighty, like an embodied vision of former times.
>
> From a considerable distance you see the dark mass of stone towering above primaeval cedars, chestnuts, oaks and limes. It stands on the rocks on the shore of the Avon, and rises to a perpendicular height of two hundred feet above the level of the water ... Going on,

you lose sight of the castle for a while, and soon find yourself before a high embattled wall, built of large blocks of stone covered by Time with moss and creeping plants. . . Suddenly, at a turn of the way, the castle starts from the wood into broad open daylight, resting on a soft grassy slope ... it is almost impossible to imagine anything more picturesque, and at the same time more imposing.

Let your fancy conjure up a space about twice as large as the interior of the Colosseum at Rome, and let it transport you into a forest of romantic luxuriance. You now overlook the large court, surrounded by mossy trees and majestic buildings, which, though of every variety of form, combine to create one sublime and connected whole, whose line,s now shooting upwards, now falling off into the blue air, with the continually changing beauty of the green earth beneath, produce, not symmetry indeed, but that *higher harmony*, else-where proper to Nature's own works alone. . . But the sublimest spectacle yet awaits you, when you raise your eyes straight before you. On this fourth side, the ground ... rises again in the form of a steep conical hill, along the sides of which climb the rugged walls of the castle ...

Figure this to yourself;—behold the whole of this magical scene at one glance;—connect with it all its associations;—think that here nine centuries of haughty power, of triumphant victory and destructive overthrow, of bloody deeds and wild greatness,—perhaps too of gentle love and noble magnanimity,—have left, in part, their visible traces, and where *they* are not, their vague romantic memory;—and then judge with what feelings I could place myself in the situation of the man to whom such recollections are daily suggested by these objects,—recollections which, to him, have all the sanctity of kindred and blood;—the man who still inhabits the very dwelling of that first possessor of the fortress of Warwick, that half-fabulous Guy, who lived a thousand years ago, and whose corroded armour, together with a hundred weapons of renowned ancestors, is preserved in the antique hall. Is there a human being so unpoetical as not to feel that the glories of such memorials, even to this very day, throw a lustre around the feeblest representative of such a race?[38]

It is clear that Pückler is drawing a parallel between his own circumstances and the landscape and dynasty of Warwick. We can detect a kind of Romantic *Sehnsucht,* a longing for a similarly august history and for an equally astonish-ing natural setting augmented by ancient architectural monuments. We can also recognize Pückler's ambition. He wants to imbue his own property with something of the same essence, even if he has to fabricate it, thereby casting a similar luster on his own person (perhaps modestly implied in the last line's ref-erence to "the feeblest representative of such a race"). Leitmotifs emerge in this letter that resonate throughout his work: imposing landscapes where nature and art combine to create beauty and impress the visitor; grand architecture; a fam-ily steeped in a politically and culturally significant past whose story speaks from every oak and from every turret; the designed landscape as history. One may be struck by Pückler's extravagance in comparing his lineage to such a ven-erable, if occasionally bloody, line of king-makers, yet the plot had already been set by the time of his crypt visit eleven years earlier. In the *Andeutungen* he men-tions Warwick again, claiming that no one could visit it without being overcome by feelings of romantic reverence, a response he wants to elicit from any visitor to Muskau.[40]

Figure 4. English house (*Andeutungen,* plate 26). Photo courtesy of the Dumbarton Oaks Research Library and Collections, Washington, DC.

Clearly Warwick was one of the places that provided mulch for the seeds of Pückler's overriding concept, yet he intended his plans for Muskau to retain, like the soil itself, a local, German character. He aspired to effects like those he admired in the British Isles, but he would achieve success by responding to his particular heritage and the site and climate of Lusatia. Even so, although he adamantly rejected the *Anglomania* that infected so many new garden designs on the Continent, Pückler did allow English elements at Muskau, several that seem to recall Warwick. Not only was there to be an English house [Fig. 4] and a ruined church, but one of Schinkel's designs was for a crenelated knights' castle on a hill overlooking the river valley, recalling Beauchamp's castle towering above the Avon. Although Pückler's castle would be artificial, dating not from the ninth but the nineteenth century, it would dominate the park's highest point, where the remains of crumbling walls, like the ancient legends, would suggest an earlier purpose. He heightens the historical, romanticized aura of the projected structure by relating two tales in the *Andeutungen.* One concerns a mysterious Russian soldier who, during the war, appeared at Muskau with an ancient map and a story of buried treasure near the ruins of a watchtower and of an underground chamber within the castle precinct, but who disappeared leaving no trace beyond the signs of an initial excavation. The second tale recounts the recent discovery not far away of a shallow grave containing a well-preserved skeleton; Pückler immediately had it buried in a simple grave adorned with an inscribed cross and a bench from which the contemplative visitor could gaze deep into a wooded ravine.[41]

Such suggestive forays into the exotic are counter-balanced, however, as he describes the panoramic view from this same hill and waxes enthusiastic about aspects of the modern world that, for him, enhance the scene: village gardens and rooftops are deemed "picturesque," and the smoke rising day and night from the chimneys of the alum works and kilns is treasured as yet another ornament, as are the pillars of fire from these same industries that illuminate the whole region each evening. In the absence of a hill, views beyond the garden were often facilitated by means of the eponymous *Pücklerschlag*, a swath cut through the trees to allow distant perspectives, a method that maintained the sense of surrounding forest while allowing the horizon to reveal the "outside" world of human activity and commerce. The knights' castle itself was not supposed to be a collapsed relic but a practical and useful structure, in effect a Romantic anachronism. Thus we may find Warwick's spirit in the enormous scale of Pückler's plans for Muskau and in his attempt to create a landscape that embodied the essence of a family and an age. Yet in the specifics of the plantings and landscaping as well as in the valuing of utility and the embrace of the bustling world beyond the garden precinct,he went his own way.

Figure 5. Neisse-Aue before park (*Andeutungen,* plate 11). Photo courtesy of the Dumbarton Oaks Research Library and Collections, Washington, DC.

The evidence of Pückler's endeavors to fashion the land includes pictorial records, such as Schinkel's architectural studies and A.W. Schirmer's illustrations for the *Andeutungen.*[42] Some of the drawings that Pückler commissioned from Schirmer were twinned views of the park, one depicting the lay-out as it existed, another that matched exactly in scale but was partly cut out to show, when super-imposed, the changes Pückler envisioned. These sketches then served as models for the printed plates in the *Andeutungen* which are bound on top of each other so that the cut-out design can be folded down or lifted away to dramatize the innovations.[43] Pückler's before-and-after views illustrate the boldness and magnitude of his plans. The most remarkable is perhaps the way he changed the village street and its environs, one of the desirable parcels of land he had managed to acquire from the original owners. In the "before" image

Figure 6. Neisse-Aue after (*Andeutungen,* plate 11). Photo courtesy of the Dumbarton Oaks
    Research Library and Collections, Washington, DC.

we see a bank raised along the Neisse and above it a street in the village of
Muskau. [Fig. 5] The transformation is revealed by folding down the irregular
flap, and the alterations give us a sense of the immensity of Pückler's schemes.
[Fig. 6] It looks, in fact, like a different scene altogether, but careful scrutiny
reveals that this is the same view: the large beech tree on the left is still there, as
is the dramatic sky, but now the river is granted a natural, graceful meander and
is widened and deepened in places so that a lake stretches out where the village
street once ran. The new landscape has also allowed deep vistas into the surrounding hills, where more distant structures are now visible through the trees.
Pückler has re-created, indeed improved upon, the natural setting that had
been disturbed by human intervention. Elsewhere at Muskau, too, riverbanks
tended to become more serpentine than they once were; indeed, whole rivers
were created, their stretches enlivened by rocky outcroppings and cascades.
One cataract may have been directly inspired by a landscape painting from the
Hudson River school rather than by the works of Claude and Poussin, which
had often been adopted as sources for picturesque gardens beginning already in
the eighteenth century.[44]

Pückler's appreciation for the dynamism of nature is apparent in all of his
writings, as is his conviction that the inherent effect of natural beauty can be
strengthened by careful human intervention: since garden art can speak nature's
universally intelligible language, a landscape park could be as immediately evocative as untouched nature. Any planned garden should accord with the *natural* setting, it should never hide but only highlight the inherent "genius of the place."
Pückler's vision was long and grandiose; his gardens were intended, like his
forests, to reach maturity only after more than a century—that is, he embraced
the rhythms of nature rather than of a human generation.[45]

His land management technique is well illustrated by his attention to trees. Trees have figured large in the German imagination,[46] and Pückler celebrated them in all manifestations, large or small, in dense forests, in isolated clumps or standing alone. For him, they seemed to represent the longevity and beauty of nature as well as ideals of individuality and of community; an exceptional specimen, such as the so-called *Hermannseiche* at Muskau, could dictate the surrounding plantings. In general, Pückler was opposed to felling trees, though they could be removed if they blocked a view or damaged the aesthetic quality of a site. Another before-and-after comparison printed in the *Andeutungen* shows that he could apply radical measures, such as the removal of twenty large lindens from in front of the palace terrace in order to open up the vista.[47]

Pückler's reverence for trees is apparent not only in his general unwillingness to fell them but in the extraordinary efforts he made to transplant them. He was, in fact, renowned for this and occasionally moved a tree or a group of trees several times before "getting it right." He transported hundreds, even thousands of trees, many over long distances and many very large.[48] The expense was enormous—not just for the moving itself. Records show that to accommodate the passage of one particularly impressive specimen, the top of the Cottbus city gate had to be removed and then replaced. There were also many bills for broken windows in various towns and villages. All in all, the trees Pückler moved had an impressive survival rate. In 1826, for example, he transplanted a forty-year old copper beach that still stands, having survived the damage Muskau suffered in the last days of the Second World War better than Schinkel's palace or the mighty lions on the terrace. In fact, it is nature that speaks most strongly from Muskau Park today. In ways not planned by Pückler, the estate exudes a sense of history through its ruins, half-destroyed bridges, overgrown paths. Time and human folly have taken their toll on the property, yet it endures, much of it still in accord with Pückler's original vision. Neither its grandeur, drama, nor historical essence attain the heights that Pückler experienced at Warwick, yet it has become a monument to its own history nonetheless and is valued on both sides of the Polish-German border, its future existence secured.

Resignation and Compromise

What was to endure was certainly a central question for Pückler. To what extent did he envision speaking to posterity in his writings and in his landscapes? It seems apparent that he was measuring himself against mighty figures such as Warwick, which is in keeping with what we understand of his ego. Yet we find expressions of resignation, if not melancholy, in Pückler's writings, signs of a conflict within his *Weltanschauung* that we also sense reflected in his approach to landscape.[49] Occasionally he ponders whether his endeavors are futile, his *Sehnsucht* perpetual—a state of uncertainty that was central to German Romantic theory but that Pückler found disheartening. As we have seen, he was not trying to create a private refuge in a never-never land, but to preserve the countryside while admitting the growth of an urban, industrial culture, maintaining what was valuable in the past while acknowledging the march of the present. He was able to imagine the new garden style helping transform Germany into what he saw as its predestined condition of freedom and equality, without altering the political structure. In his mind, political union was something quite separate from national identity, and not necessarily desirable in its own right. In this respect the realization of a national identity was best accomplished at the level of cultural consciousness. Hence, the noble landowner, prince, or city official dutifully builds a new garden to inspire and educate the population. Cultivation of the garden means cultivation of the self and brings enlightenment, happiness and a better life for all. And yet, would such an ambition be realized?

Pückler describes a moment during his visit to Warwick where he lapsed into a kind of reverie before a Titian portrait of Machiavelli, and his account betrays an almost schizophrenic clash of admiration and derision for both Machiavelli and the human condition.

> Precisely as I should imagine him. A face of great acuteness and prudence, and of suffering,—as if lamenting over the profoundly-studied worthless side of human nature; that hound-like character which loves where it is spurned, follows where it fears, and is faithful where it is fed. A trace of compassionate scorn plays round the thin lips, while the dark eye appears turned reflectingly inward.... It appears strange, at first sight, that this great and classic writer should so long have been misunderstood in the grossest manner.... On more attentive observation, we arrive at the conviction that it was reserved for modern times, in which politics at length begin to be viewed and understood from a higher and really humane point of view, to form a correct judgement of Machiavel's Prince.

Although initially ambivalent, Pückler goes on to take a position on the evils of arbitrary power, and with a hint of sarcasm disassociates himself from such unfeeling tyrants—among them Napoleon, who is subtly mocked for his inability to understand the lessons of the true tyrant, Machiavelli:

> To all arbitrary princes—and under that name I class all those who think themselves invested with power solely 'par la grâce de Dieu' and for their own advantage,—all conquerors, and children of fortune, whom some chance has given to the people they regard as their property,—to all such as these, this profound and acute writer shows the true and only way to prosper; the exhaustive system they must of necessity follow, in order to maintain a power radically sprung from the soil of sin and error. His book is, and must ever be, the true, inimitable gospel of such rulers; and we Prussians, especially, have reason to congratulate ourselves that Napoleon had learned his Machiavel so ill;—we should otherwise probably be still groaning under his yoke.
>
> That Machiavel felt all the value and the power of freedom is plain, from many passages in his book. In one he says, 'He who has conquered a *free* city, has no secure means of keeping it, but either to destroy it, or to people it with new inhabitants; *for no benefit a sovereign can confer will ever make it forget its lost freedom.*'

By proving, as he incontestably does, that such a degree of arbitrary power can be maintained only by the utter disregard of all morality, and by seriously inculcating this doctrine upon princes, he also demonstrates but too plainly, that the whole frame of society, in his time, contained within itself a principle of demoralization; and that no true happiness, no true civilization, was possible to any people till that principle was detected and destroyed. The events of modern times, and their consequences, have at length opened their eyes to this truth, and they will not close them again![50]

Pückler insists there is no turning back; "true civilization" has destroyed the possibility of another Machiavelli. Yet he is not calling for a revolution here, nor does he feel a violent change in the political or social structure is necessary. Rather he is convinced that the current state of affairs in Germany allows him, as an enlightened and benevolent ruler, to create a garden and a social paradise for himself and his subjects, a realm where freedom and nature reign.[51] The way is open for a prince committed to virtue. Yet Pückler was conscious of his own precarious position in a society that was inexorably changing; could the benefits of the English model be achieved within the system practiced by the German ruling class? The ideals of the time that he saw reflected in the German lands seemed to leave ample room for personal expression as well as for measured criticism of the existing system.[52] He was not unaware of the political implications of the new garden style but he was, at times, disheartened at the lack of appreciation he encountered for it. In a letter dated September 26, 1827, not quite a year after his Warwick visit, he indulges in a moment of cynicism as he draws a comparison between the pacific creativity of his own endeavors and Napoleon's much noisier successes. Although both men spend time drawing up plans, he writes, his own are for gardens, Napoleon's for victories on the battlefield and on the world stage: "He, however, with his rough pencil drew blood; I only water and flower-beds;— he fortifications, I summer houses; he soldiers, and I trees." And he concludes: "In the sight of the All-seeing it may be the same whether his children play with cannon-balls or with nuts; but to men the difference is considerable: in their opinion, he who causes them to be shot by thousands is far greater than he who only labours to promote their enjoyment."[53] This is flat-out discontent, even disgust. We also hear an echo of the disillusionment with human nature that he expressed in the earlier passage on Machiavelli.

In other ways, too, the essential optimism in the scope and vitality of Pückler's undertakings cannot always mask a tone of despondency. At one point in the *Andeutungen* he voices a melancholic, if droll, regret that time is moving too fast, that "the *Zeitgeist* is truly wearing seven-league boots."[54] That is, Pückler felt political realities, like the economic realities of his own situation, impinging on him in uncomfortable ways. He foresaw the changes the industrial revolution would bring to Germany. And he clearly perceived the shifts in political power that were already occurring. An old way of life was threatened with obliteration just as the natural landscape itself was in danger of being overrun. He saw his contribution in danger of being dismissed, the "poetry" of the nobleman's legacy losing out to a new economic standard: "You now have the money and the power. Let the poor, used-up nobility have its poetry—the only thing left to it. Honor weak old age, you Spartans!"⁵⁵ This from a thirty-year old! In 1848, when the revolutionary spirit took temporary hold in Germany, Pückler responded by maintaining his equivocal stance: he admired the new republican determination to establish a parliament and a constitution, yet he still associated with and admired the Prussian royal family and much of what it stood for. In the end he despaired of both sides and ultimately retreated from the fray, choosing to be absorbed in his gardens and his travels. He begins to look something of a latter-day Candide.

Figure 7. "Begräbnisscapelle," a burial chapel by Schinkel (*Andeutungen,* plate 28). Photo courtesy of the Dumbarton Oaks Research Library and Collections, Washington, DC.

Pückler self-consciously set out to create a legacy, and indeed more than that, to create his own myth. He envisioned a worthy resting place for his revered ancestors and for himself, a *Begräbnisscapelle* (burial chapel). This was one of the buildings that Schinkel would eventually design for Muskau Park. [Fig. 7] The imposing structure was intended to rise on a broad terrace from where it could be seen from the palace, thus serving as an ever-present memento mori. Its main purpose was as a burial place for the Pückler family, although the local Catholic population, who otherwise had to travel two miles to a service, would be allowed to use it as their house of worship. The chapel was to include an eclectic array of architectural and painted features such as windows from the old city church at Boppart am Rhein, a Crucifixion by Martin van Heemskerk the Elder, statues of Poetry and Philosophy, and a pre-Christian altar discovered somewhere on the Muskau estate. Even though, like a number of the other buildings described and illustrated in the *Andeutungen,* this structure was never built, Pückler did succeed much later in erecting a burial site that is itself a powerfully evocative memento mori, a reminder of death that Pückler felt could be profitably viewed every day, since "for every thinking person" the feelings evoked should never be disheartening."[56] This is the second of the two grass- and vine-covered pyramids he constructed in his later years on the grounds of Branitz. The first is a large land pyramid that seems less reminiscent of Egyptian pyramids, which Pückler did experience, than of pre-Columbian structures (of which he could have read or seen in stage designs by Schinkel), though it also recalls ancient Germanic grave mounds. Even larger is the tumulus—a pyramid sixty feet high and one hundred twenty feet wide which rises from a lake in the mode of the massive wonders described by Herodotus. [Fig. 8] This he designed as the final resting place for himself and Lucie. He intended both structures simply to stand imposingly, to make—like mountains—their own statement; to last forever.[57]

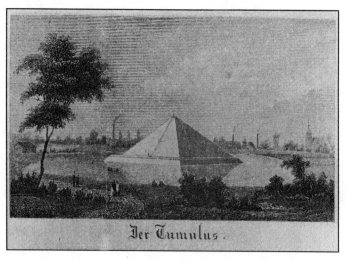

Figure 8. The "Tumulus." Steel engraving by Poppel & Kurz after a drawing by Gottheil, 1857. Photo courtesy of the Archiv der Stiftung Fürst-Pückler-Museum Park und Schloss Branitz.

The intriguing resonance between Pückler-Muskau's designs upon his land and the preoccupations of the central characters in Goethe's *Die Wahlverwandtschaften* is provacative.[58] The making of great parks is the leitmotif in Pückler-Muskau's biography, the foil against which he played out his life. In the process, the park came to conceptualize many things as a place and an idea, its power exercised through its visible presence as locality and through its fictional existence as text. Whether such a creation might be possible is one of the central questions raised in Goethe's novel, and the answer is unclear, since that garden's beauty is at once life-giving and simultaneously a setting for death and lamentation. As its owner Eduard finally despairs that his whole life has been a self-deception, a mere imitation, the reader must wonder to what extent his garden was similarly insubstantial. Muskau Park is itself to a large extent a fiction. That is, it exists in literary reality in the *Andeutungen*—described in words and in lithographs—but much of that ideal landscape garden was never realized.

For Pückler, as for Eduard, the creation of a landscape was a process of self-definition, the social and artistic construction of a private and public identity. Pückler expresses this tension in the *Andeutungen* as he explains his fundamental vision for Muskau:

> The central idea that I made the basis of my entire plan was just this: to create an appropriate image of the life of our family, or of the local patriciate, and how it developed here, and to do so in such a way that this idea would arise, as it were, on its own in the viewer's mind. All that was needed was to make use of what was already there, to highlight and thus enrich it, but to do no violence to the locality or its history. Many ultra-liberals will perhaps smile at such a thought, but every type of human development is honorable, and perhaps because the one discussed here may be approaching its demise, it is beginning to become generally, poetically, and romantically interesting again in a way that factories, machines, and even constitutions cannot yet claim.[59]

This is consistent with his organic model of community, an ideal that supports him in his later estrangement from the political arena. English garden design and the English democratic model are overlain with romanticism and with what some would still say was a German proclivity to philosophize more than to engage. Earlier in the same text Pückler explains how any large landscape design must be based on a *Grund-Idee*, a fundamental and consistent notion that is developed and executed by a single, directing hand. He goes on to elaborate on his particular use of the term *Idee*: "An idea in its higher meaning is also fundamental to garden-landscape-art in general, namely: to create out of the whole landscape of nature a concentrated picture, a kind of nature in miniature as a poetic ideal—the same idea that in other realms gives essence to every true work of art and that has made out of man himself a microcosm."[60] The garden artist is guided by personal circumstances—aspects of his own life, of his family history, of the region; these form the basis on which his fantasy and creativity take root.

Pückler wanted both his park and his life to reflect a utopian model of aristocratic society. His vision was not simply aesthetic or ecological but also political, sociological, and historical. Yet the tantalizing portrait Pückler has left us is elusive. The implied veracity of the descriptions in the *Andeutungen* is at odds with the garden as realized. Rather, Pückler established it as a metaphor, a figure representing the apprehensible present, the implied past, and the promise of the future, the state of always becoming, *das immer Werdende*. He himself recognized that there could be nothing better than a garden to embody this central Romantic trope—whether created out of nature or out of words and visual images.[61] There is a striking moment near the end of *Die Wahlverwandtschaften* where Goethe allows the great landscape park fashioned by his protagonists to cease "becoming." This occurs when its last visitor, an Englishman, walks through it with a camera obscura, capturing each scene as if recording a succession of framed views suitable for painting, making the garden a model but snuffing out its life, its capacity for further effect and change. Yet it does, of course, continue to grow and change in the reader's imagination. Similarly Pückler's gardens, as both text and not-text, were both constant and always evolving, in words, in our imagination, and in the living, natural landscape.

Pückler's varied legacy is a demonstration of his faith in the durability of his creations, be they in the form of texts, gardens, or myths. He acknowledged early that an artist's imagination can create a beauty and truth of its own that surpasses reality. In 1832, he received a letter from a childhood friend who, transported by the descriptions in Pückler's *Briefe,* laments that in his own life he has seen the earth's full beauty only in his dreams. To this Pückler responds with a reassurance: "At most the traveler sees and learns; he leafs through a picture book. Creative genius, however, invents its own world out of inner knowledge, concocts and paints the glorious pictures that bring joy to thousands and thousands who thereby learn to know the world, and themselves, more deeply."[62]

Notes

1. Pückler was granted the title *Fürst* (prince) in 1822 at the time that his Prussian territories were diminished and his prerogatives in local rule curtailed. A published account from 1800 describes the realm as over nine square miles in extent with more than forty small villages beyond the *Städtchen* of Muskau and with a population of 8,534. See Karl August Engelhardt, "Die freie Standesherrschaft Muskau," in *Erdbeschreibung der Markgrafthümer Ober- und Niederlausitz* (Leipzig, 1800): reprinted in *Im Spiegel der Erinnerung. Hermann Fürst von Pückler-Muskau: Gartenkünstler Schriftsteller Weltenbummler* (Branitz, 1995), 12-17.

2. There are scenes in Hoffmann's "Phantasienstücken in Callots Manier" that are reminiscent of this event and may well have been inspired by Pückler, who was a close acquaintance of the writer.

3. This is an impressive, if doubtful, heritage. Pückler admits to the shakiness of the proof, adding "who would hold it against us that we place high value on being, thanks to our ancestors, so romantically linked to the immortal heroic epic of the German people, even if we only have probability on our side." Pückler-Muskau, *Andeutungen über Landschaftsgärtnerei* (1834: reprint Stuttgart, 1977), 87. All English translations from this text are my own.

4. See, for instance, Siegmar Gerndt, *Idealisierte Natur: die literarische Kontroverse um den Landschaftsgarten des 18. und frühen 19. Jahrhunderts in Deutschland* (Stuttgart, 1981), 146.

5. Walter Benjamin, "Goethes 'Wahlverwandtschaften,'" in *Spiegelungen Goethes in unserer Zeit,* ed. Hans Mayer (Wiesbaden, 1949), 11-93.

6. Pückler was acquainted with many leading figures on the German cultural scene including Goethe, who wrote a glowing review of Pückler's *Briefe eines Verstorbenen* (see below note 19) and who encouraged the Prince in his landscape gardening pursuits. He was a friend and patron of artists such as Friedrich Schinkel, of cultural and political figures such as Rahel and Karl August Varnhagen, and of writers such as Brentano and Heine, the latter of whom dubbed him the "last knight of the old landed aristocracy" and lauded him for lecturing the upstarts of the new aristocracy on the subject of honor. See Heinz Ohff, *Der grüne Fürst. Das abenteuerliche Leben des Hermann Pückler-Muskau* (München & Zurich, 1993), 276. He knew

and upon occasion sparred with the other German landscapists of his time. He expressed the hope that Lenné would transform Potsdam into an appropriately German landscape that could rival English parks, but in general he found little to admire in the landscape design practiced in his native land; no real "nature-painting" but rather a willingness to order a garden as one would order a new piece of clothing from a tailor. Pückler-Muskau, *Andeutungen*, 15.

7. C.C.L. Hirschfeld, *Theorie der Gartenkunst*, 5 vols., (Leipzig, 1779-85); reprinted in reduced facsimile, five volumes in two, with an introduction by Hans Foramitti (Hildesheim, Zurich, and New York, 1973 and 1985). English translation: *Theory of Garden Art*, edited and translated by Linda B. Parshall (Philadelphia, 2001). All references are to the English edition.

8. Hirschfeld, *Theory*, 98-100.

9. For instance, Pückler names two linden-lined walks after local figures of prominence, a philosopher Grävell and the poet Leopold Schefer. *Andeutungen*, 113.

10. Joseph Rückert uses this expression in a description of Weimar Park, *Bemerkungen über Weimar 1799*, reprinted with an afterword by Eberhard Haufe (Weimar, 1969), 25.

11. Some even saw the garden revolution as capable of achieving the results in Germany that political revolution had in France. See Gerndt, *Idealisierte Natur*, 116-18, for some examples of this thinking. For the political implications of nature and gardens in revolutionary France, see Hans-Christian and Elke Harten, *Die Versöhnung mit der Natur. Gärten, Freiheitsbäume, republikanische Wälder, heilige Berge und Tugendparks in der Französischen Revolution* (Hamburg, 1989).

12. His weakness for and success with women are major leitmotifs for Pückler's biographers. August Jäger clearly admired and sympathized with him, interjecting an unusually personal note in claiming "in my opinion pretty girls should be banned from University towns, since they definitely keep people from their studies." See Jäger, *Das Leben des Fürsten von Pückler-Muskau* (Stuttgart, 1943); reprinted in *Im Spiegel der Erinnerung*, 24.

13. Ibid., 40. Jäger claims Pückler was "always in the front lines" in these conflicts—phrasing that recalls the praise of Hildebrand in the *Hildebrandslied*, an allusion that would have delighted Pückler.

14. This area was self-consciously proud of its local heritage and celebrated the ancient graves in the area. See a 1832 letter to Pückler by Friedrich Förster published in Pückler-Muskau, *Briefwechsel und Tagebücher des Fürsten Hermann von Pückler-Muskau*, edited by Ludmilla Assing (vols. 1-2 Hamburg, 1873; vols. 3-9 Berlin, 1874-1876; repr. Bern, 1971), 7: 434.

15. Ibid., 432.

16. The park now extends over only 545 hectares. Since the Neisse was established as a political border after World War II, about 200 hectares of the park lie in Germany and the remainder in Poland.

17. As he did with garden views, Pückler provided before-and-after maps of the property in the *Andeutungen*. Only one-third of his projected plans were accomplished by the time he had to sell the property in 1845. See Manfred Uhlitz, "Prince Pückler and John Adey Repton's Visit to Prussia," *Journal of Garden History* 9 (1989): 229.

18. He paid a reputedly minor honey tax to the estate. This and the other statistics about the Muskau economy are found in Engelhardt, "Die freie Standesherrschaft."

19. Pückler-Muskau, *Briefe eines Verstorbenen* (published anonymously in four volumes, 1830-31; new edition ed. by Heinz Ohff, Berlin, 1986), 553. A four-volume English translation by an unnamed Sarah Austin appeared quickly after the publication of the original German edition: *Tour in England, Ireland, and France in the Years 1828 & 1829*, vols. 1 & 2; and *Tour in Germany, Holland and England in the years 1826, 1827, & 1828, In a series of letters by a German Prince*, vols. 3 & 4 (London, 1832). All quotations here from the *Briefe* are taken from Austin's translation.

20. Hirschfeld, *Theory*, p. 149.

21. *Tour*, III: 253-54 (*Briefe*, 553). Blenheim provided a model for Pückler in its grandeur but also in the difficulty of its upkeep, which Thomas Jefferson commented on when he visited it in

the 1780s, noting that all together two hundred gardeners were kept busy there, and that the grass required mowing every ten days; see John Dixon Hunt and Peter Willis, eds., *Genius of the Place* (London, 1975), 336.

22. *Tour,* I: 312 (*Briefe,* 174).

23. Hirschfeld, *Theory,* 148. This combination of nature and art was an essential principle for the leading English theorists of the time such as Thomas Whately, Horace Walpole ,and Humphry Repton.

24. See Karl Eduard Petzold, *Fürst Hermann von Pückler-Muskau in seinem Wirken in Muskau und Branitz, Eine biographische Skizze* (Leipzig, 1874), 10-12.

25. Goldsmith was presumably referring to the destruction of a village at Nuneham Park; this seemingly hardhearted practice happened elsewhere in England as well, such as at Richmond Park, where Brown had the village of West Sheen removed to improve the vistas. It has been argued that sometimes a new, planned village was provided not far away for the displaced families. See Ann Bermingham, *Landscape and Ideology.: The English Rustic Tradition, 1740-1860* (Berkeley & Los Angeles, 1986), 11.

26. In the published letters he addresses her as "Julie"—surely an allusion to Rousseau's *La Nouvelle Heloise.*

27. He even sent for his head gardener from Muskau, Jacob Heinrich Rehder, so the two could tour the gardens of southern England together. Rehder stayed on at Muskau after its sale in 1845, working for the new owners until his death in 1852. Both he and his successor, Eduard Petzold, continued to developed the garden in accordance with Pückler's original vision. Rehder's grandson Alfred was himself a gardener for over five decades at the Arnold Arboretum of Harvard University. See Gerhard Rehder, "The Making of a Botanist," *Arnoldia,* 32 (1972): 141-56.

28. See note 19 above.

29. Byron had many admirers in Germany who scorned the English for failing to appreciate him. Pückler did not sanction the criticism he heard in England, claiming "the soul of a poet like Byron is hard to judge;—the ordinary standard is quite inadequate to it, and very few people have any other to apply." *Tour,* IV: 148 (*Briefe,* 721). There are tempting similarities between Pückler and the English poet: both were known for their outrageous behavior; Byron, too, claimed to have edited out "*all* the really *consequential* and *important* parts" from his memoirs (see *Lord Byron, Selected Letters and Journals,* ed. L.A. Marchand, [Cambridge, 1982]); and each man clearly enjoyed his own company.

30. See Pückler-Muskau, *Aus Mehemed Alis Reich. Ägypten und der Sudan um 1840* (Stuttgart, 1844)*;* reprint with an afterword by Günther Jantzen (Zurich, 1985), 501-2 (a paragraph headed "Nicht für Damen," "not for ladies"); 659 (a paragraph headed "Nicht für Damen und nur für Naturforscher," "not for ladies and only for naturalists"); and 678 (one paragraph printed upside-down with no special heading).

31. His books include: *Tutti Frutti,* 5 vols. (Stuttgart, 1834); *Jugend-Wanderungen* (Stuttgart, 1835); *Vorletzter Weltgang von Semilasso,* 3 vols. (Stuttgart, 1835); *Semilasso in Afrika,* 5 vols. (Stuttgart, 1836); *Der Vorläufer* (Stuttgart, 1838)*; Südöstlicher Bildersaal,* 3 vols. (Stuttgart, 1840-41); *Aus Mehemed Alis Reich,* 3 vols. (Stuttgart, 1844); *Der Rückkehr,* 3 vols. (Berlin 1846-48). See also Assing, ed., *Briefwechsel und Tagebücher* (note 14 above) for selections from his letters and diaries.

32. See note 6 above. This publication was in his mind already in 1825; see Norbert Miller, "Die beseelte Natur. Der literarische Garten und die Theorie der Landschaft nach 1800," in Helmut Pfotenhauer, ed., *Kunstliteratur als Italienerfahrung* (Tübingen, 1991), 154.

33. At Göttingen University, there were two professors who taught courses in the art of traveling. See David Blackbourn, *The Long Nineteenth Century:. A History of Germany, 1780-1918* (Oxford & New York, 1997), 35-6.

34. See Patrick Bowe, "Pückler-Muskau's Estate and its Influence on American Landscape Architecture," *Garden History* 23 (1995): 192-200. Bowe points out Pückler's significant influence

on this second generation of American landscape designers. Eliot, a Boston landscape architect who was apprenticed to Olmstead, visited Muskau in 1886 and wrote: "Altogether it is the most remarkable and lovable park I have seen on the Continent.... The work of Fürst Pückler is of a sort to make me very proud of my profession" (quoted in Bowe, 194).

35. Petzold (1815-91) published a number of books and articles on gardens in general and specifically about Muskau, for example *Der Park von Muskau. Für Freunde der Landschaftsgärtnerei und den Fremden zum Wegweiser* (Hoyerswerda, 1856) and *Fürst Hermann v. Pückler-Muskau* (1874: cited above). On Petzold see Michael Rohde, *Von Muskau bis Konstantinopel. Eduard Petzold, ein europäischer Gartenkünstler, 1815-1891* (Dresden, 1998). For a chronological list of events from the history of both Muskau and Branitz, including specifics about major plantings, structures, repairs, etc., see "Chronologische Fakten" in Helmut Rippl, ed., *Der Parkschöpfer Pückler-Muskau: das gartenkünstlerische Erbe des Fürsten Hermann Ludwig Heinrich von Pückler-Muskau* (Weimar, 1995), 231-49; this volume is a new, extensively revised edition of Joachim Fait & Detlef Karg, eds., *Hermann Ludwig Heinrich Fürst von Pückler-Muskau. Gartenkunst und Denkmalpflege* (Weimar, 1989). Another detailed look at the history of Muskau is given in Hermann Graf von Arnim and Willi A. Boelcke, *Muskau. Standesherrschaft zwischen Spree und Neiße* (Frankfurt/Main, & Berlin, 1992); this is a reprint, with additional material (492-a-d), of a 1978 publication. The Arnim family acquired Muskau in 1883.

36. The story of his relationship with his English translator, Sarah Austin, is a fascinating one. Her sensitivity to his prose, her own literary gifts, and her careful expurgating of certain potentially damaging passages were crucial to his English success. See Lotte and Joseph Hamburger, eds., *Contemplating Adultery: The Secret Life of a Victorian Woman* (New York, 1991). There is also a short account of her relationship with Pückler in the introduction to E.M. Butler's abridged edition of her translation: *A Regency Visitor. The English Tour of Prince Pückler-Muskau Described in his Letters, 1826-1828* (New York, 1958).

37. Sarah Austin's translation renders Pückler's term *Zauberwort* as "enchanted palace," thereby missing what is certainly a reference to the famous lines from Eichendorff's poem "Wünschelrute" in which the poetic spirit can bring the world itself to sing: "Schläft ein Lied in allen Dingen, / Die da träumen fort und fort, / Und die Welt hebt an zu singen, / Triffst du nur das Zauberwort."

38. *Tour*, III: 210-15 (*Briefe*, 527ff.).

39. The powerful Earl of Warwick referred to here is not Richard de Beauchamp but his son-in-law, Richard Neville. The gardens that Pückler saw were designed by "Capability" Brown for Francis Greville, Earl Brooke. The Greville family, distantly related to the Beauchamps, acquired Warwick Castle in 1604.

40. *Andeutungen*, 30.

41. *Andeutungen*, 81, 127.

42. Pückler commissioned a whole series of drawings from Schirmer, a young Berlin landscape painter.

43. This method of producing before-and-after views was introduced by Humphrey Repton (1752-1818), the major English landscape gardener of the era. Repton was famous for his red-bound books, which he prepared for his clients so they could see how their gardens would be transformed. Rousseau's friend Girardin did something similar for his garden at Ermenonville. See Marie Luise Gothein, *Geschichte der Gartenkunst* II (Jena, 1914), 319. Pückler, unaware that Repton had died in 1818, invited him to Muskau in 1821 to help design the park; his son and successor, John Adey Repton, showed up instead. See Uhlitz, "Prince Pückler and John Adey Repton's Visit to Prussia," 221-30.

Later drawings as well as other written documentation survive. Pückler's gardeners, Georg Christoph Bleyer (1837-1915) at Branitz and Jacob Heinrich Rehder and Eduard Petzold at Muskau, continued to execute Pückler's plans even after his death, and Petzold left lengthy written and visual records of his work. See note 35 above.

44. See Joachim Wolschke-Bulmahn, "Zwischen Hudson-River und Neiße. Fürst Pückler, die Muskauer Wasserfälle und das Hudson-River-Portfolio," *Gartenkunst* 19 (1998): 300-09.

45. At one point in the *Andeutungen,* he takes Hirschfeld's argument for the priority of garden art and expands it in an interesting direction, comparing landscape art with drama:

"The highest degree of landscape garden art is reached only where it appears to be nothing but free nature in her noblest form. This Painting with Nature has an essential affinity with the dramatic arts, for both are unique in using nature itself as both material and object of representation. . . . The comparison goes further, in that both art forms are very precarious, but the garden artist has the advantage. Still, one could perhaps compare landscape art with music and, since architecture has been termed 'frozen music,' landscape art might be called 'vegetating music.' It too has its symphonies, its adagios and allegros, and all have the same deep effect on the soul." *Andeutungen,* 76.

46. The eighteenth century even drew a parallel between freedom for plants and for man. Schiller, a gardener's son, wrote about the rights of the individual tree. See Hirschfeld, *Theory,* 25-26.

47. *Andeutungen,* plates II a and II b. In a chapter on "Moving Large Trees and Their Grouping," he bemoans the unnecessary felling of trees, although he confesses to himself having removed eighty thus far. Elsewhere, for instance at Neu Hardenberg, his father-in-law's estates, he seems to have been more ruthless, having around eight hundred trees felled within a short period. See Uhlitz, "Prince Pückler and John Adey Repton's Visit to Prussia," 206.

48. Just for the park at Branitz—only one-eighth the size of Muskau—Pückler planted tens of thousands of trees and moved four hundred large specimens, some from many miles away; see Ohff, *Der grüne Fürst,* 261ff. An article in the *Washington Post* (8 October 1999) reported on the current status value of trees (bigger tree equals bigger status symbol) and the companies that charge enormous fees for providing full-grown specimens. For instance a thirty-foot tree cost $20,000 in late 1999, and the price rose to $60,000 with the installation and insurance charges included. If only Pückler could have charged such fees for his services, he might have salvaged his beloved Muskau. Interestingly, the work is done today mostly in the same way as in Pückler's time, namely a skilled worker digs the root ball (it still takes a full day); this is covered with burlap, bound with rope, and the tree is then hoisted onto a cart or truck.

49. A recent study examines Pückler's melancholic views: Ulf Jacob, "'Ich möchte manchmal ganz sehnlich, ich wäre todt.' Andeutungen über das Melancholische in Hermann Fürst von Pückler-Muskaus Persönlichkeit und künstlerischem Werk," in *Pückler—Pyramiden—Panorama* (Cottbus, 1999), 110-24.

50. The Machiavelli passages are found in *Tour,* III: 218-20 (*Briefe,* 531-2).

51. At Muskau, he not only answered Hirschfeld's call for a garden in the natural style, but he engaged his subjects in creating and maintaining it, participating in it, and he made it open to all and sundry, another of Hirschfeld's appeals. See Hirschfeld, *Theory,* 226-27.

52. Censorship, serfdom, lack of individual freedoms—all these were being openly discussed, criticized, and gradually transformed in the Germany of his day. Civil rights, education, etc. were concerns of Pückler's too, as we have seen. Yet even though there was no revolution as such in Germany, society was advancing in ways that removed power from the princes. Pückler scorned the monarchy but did not think the German people were capable of governing themselves. The failure of the revolution in 1848 confirmed his feelings. He claimed that although it was natural for an Englishman or Frenchman to be a patriot, the only sensible option for a modern German was to be a cosmopolitan. See Ian Buruma, *Anglomania. A European Love Affair* (New York, 1998), 99.

53. *Tour,* IV: 157 (*Briefe,* 726), letter of 5 September.

54. *Andeutungen,* 79. The reference is to the loss of his rights within his Prussian territories.

55. *Andeutungen,* 84. Later, after having been forced from Muskau and after the 1848 revolution, he wrote to Ludmilla Assing, his biographer, in a similar tone, resigned to having his ideas realized only by later generations. See Detlef Kar, "Der Muskauer Park—ein Werk des Fürsten Hermann von Pückler—Vergangenheit, Gegenwart und Zukunft," *Gartenkunst* 2 (1990): 63.

56. Pückler expresses these thoughts in his discussion of the family burial chapel planned for Muskau: see *Andeutungen,* 113.
57. For articles on Pückler's pyramids and their connections with Egypt, the Koran, Freemasonry, and other exotic sources, see *Pückler—Pyramiden—Panorama* (Cottbus, 1999).
58. In each case, an ancestral estate is transformed into a landscape park that comes to allegorize the essential moral, aesthetic and social threads of human life. Both deal with past and present, with ideality versus reality, with passion for and in the landscape. Both face the problem of incorporating villages and villagers into a large estate. Chapels and graveyards make significant appearances in both. Goethe, too, was influenced by Repton. See Miller, "Die beseelte Natur," 123.
59. *Andeutungen,* 84.
60. *Andeutungen,* 18.
61. For this pregnant and essential phrase, one of the core tenets of German Romanticism, he quotes the Romantic philosopher Fichte's comment on the German language. Pückler claims the advantage of such potentiality for gardens which, by definition, can never be finished: *Andeutungen,* 70. Friedrich Schlegel earlier expanded on the image, so apt for gardens: "Romantic poetry is still becoming; yes, that is its essence, that it must always only become, can never be completed"; August Wilhelm and Friedrich Schlegel, eds., *Athenaeum* (1798-1800), Fragment Number 116.
62. This exchange of letters between Pückler and a certain Houwald is printed in *Briefwechsel und Tagebücher* 7: 435-38.

Chapter 4

ALL OF GERMANY A GARDEN?
Changing Ideas of Wilderness in German Garden Design
and Landscape Architecture

Joachim Wolschke-Bulmahn

"Wilderness" has become a topic of increasing scholarly discussion over the past two decades. Stimulated by concern with worldwide environmental problems and renewed reflection on the relationship between human beings and the natural world, this scholarly interest is attested to by books such as Max Oelschlaeger's *The Idea of Wilderness*, Simon Schama's *Landscape and Memory*, and the collection *Schön wild sollte es sein* edited by the Bavarian Academy for Nature Preservation and Landscape Care.[1]

I use the term "wilderness" here in a general way, following the several definitions given in *Chambers Twentieth-Century Dictionary*—among them "a region uncultivated and uninhabited: a pathless or desolate tract of any kind" and, more specifically with reference to garden art, "a part of a garden or estate allowed to run wild, or cultivated in imitation of natural woodland."[2] Definitions of the term "wild" run from "being in a state of nature, not tamed or cultivated" through "of an undomesticated or uncultivated kind" to "uncivilized, uninhabited, desolate."[3] "Wilderness" can thus refer to uncultivated, uninhabited regions and desolate landscapes as well as to parts of gardens and parks that have been designed as an artistic expression of nature.

Garden and Wilderness in the Renaissance

The garden and the idea of the garden were almost antithetical to the concept of wilderness in the early periods of horticulture and garden art. The garden,

Notes for this section begin on page 90.

enclosed by a fence or wall, had to be demarcated from and protected against hostile and invasive nature. It was created to offer protection against nature, a place where nature was transformed, where it was tamed and ordered. Though originally set up to help ensure survival through the cultivation of vegetables and fruit, the garden over time became a place for artistic transformation and representation of nature. The *hortus conclusus* of the Middle Ages is representative of this development of the garden and the relationship between mankind, nature, and wilderness.[4] Although there was already an aesthetic appreciation of "landscape" outside the garden,[5] the *hortus conclusus*, the garden as protection against wild nature, remained the dominant symbol for the times. "From the governing medieval Christian perspective, wild nature had to be tamed, and thereby civilized or brought into harmony with the divine order," Oelschlaeger writes.[6] "To revere wild nature was, to the medieval mind, a blatant heresy. By taming the wilderness the holy brothers fulfilled God's plan, simultaneously exercising human dominion over nature and exterminating paganism."[7]

The Renaissance was a time of important change in the relationship between mankind and nature. According to Oelschlaeger, it "led to the wholesale conversion of first the European, and then the American wilderness into civilization."[8] Beginning with the Renaissance, the artistic depiction of nature and wilderness within the garden gradually gained in significance as an expression of the increasing domination over nature and, probably, as an early manifestation of longing for wild nature because of man's encroachment on it. The garden became an artistic representation of the whole world—and that included wilderness.

The Renaissance was not only a time of rediscovery and adaptation of the ideas and ideals of antiquity but also a time of scientific discoveries, of an explosion of knowledge and, concurrently, of a new perception and understanding of the world. The Renaissance universe, according to Claudia Lazarro, was,

> hierarchical, with God at the summit, human beings in the center, nature below, and each part related to the other. The natural world was perceived in terms of its usefulness for human needs; plants and animals provide food and medicine. They also reflect human traits, virtues, and beliefs, and serve therefore as symbols—heraldic, moral, philosophical, and religious. At the same time, the visible world corresponds with the divinely created cosmos; the microcosm reflects the macrocosm. To know this world is therefore also to know God. Finally, some forces in nature can be manipulated and controlled to benefit human life, while others remain uncontrollable. All these aspects of mankind's relationship with nature were exhibited in Renaissance gardens, in the planting, design, and sculpted ornamentation, but also in earth moving, hydraulics, and water-powered devices.[9]

The garden occupies a very special place in Renaissance thought: as a work of art, as an imitation of nature, and also as a new nature in its own right:

> In antiquity, as in the Renaissance, the interaction of human culture and the natural world was expressed through the paired concepts of art and nature. The dialogue between art and nature was by no means limited to gardens, but was particularly appropriate to them....

Garden design rested on the principle that art imitates nature; but in the playful spirit of these realms of green, nature also 'imitates her imitator art.' A valley made by nature seemed instead made by art; a cave presented a puzzle: was it carved from the mountain naturally, or manually? In the eyes of contemporaries, art's intervention was not always distinguishable from nature's creation, and this confusion was manifest throughout the garden . . . A garden similarly manifests the rivalry between its two essential aspects, not the victory of one over the other, since 'life-giving nature never wins, nor art either.' Art might seem to triumph over its competitor, as at the Villa d'Este at Tivoli, where 'nature agrees to confess to having been surpassed by art' or so an admirer claimed in his compliment to its owner and creator, Cardinal Ippolito d'Este.[10]

Out of this interaction of art and nature evolved the concept of the garden as a third nature. It was "a couple of Italian humanists who offered one of the most interesting conceptual handles on garden art," John Dixon Hunt writes. "Independently of each other, or so it seems, Bartolomeo Taegio and Jacopo Bonfadio coined the same term for gardens: a 'third nature.'"[11] The garden as a third nature meant that nature and art develop into an unmistakable whole, that they enter into a symbiotic relationship and produce something new which is neither nature nor art. This idea has its roots in antiquity; the expression was used to describe human modification of the natural environment. Cicero explained the process in *De natura deorum*: "We sow corn and plant trees. We fertilize the soil by irrigation. We dam the rivers, to guide them where we will. One may say that we seek with our human hands to create a second nature in the natural world."[12]

The idea of a third nature that, unifying art and nature, conceived of the garden as a representation of the world was a new and fundamental aspect of the Renaissance garden. Nature, the natural environment of the garden, and particular fea-

Figure 1. Artificial hill with grotto. From Salomon de Caus, Von *gewaltsamen Bewegungen* (1615), Book II.

tures of nature became a theme for garden art. As part of this development, wilderness also gained relevance for garden art. Art imitated nature in the Renaissance garden, and advances in science and technology supported this development. It is reflected in artificial-looking grottoes and artificial hills that were intended to represent natural mountains [Figure 1]; in artificial rain showers and sculptures that symbolized rivers [Figure 2]; and in the inclusion of the animal world through sculptures, automata, or live creatures (e.g., in aviaries) [Figure 3]. Artificial wildernesses were integrated in gardens as an artistic representation of nature.[13]

Figure 2. Sculpture representing a river. From Salomon de Caus, *Von gewaltsamen Bewegungen* (1615), Book II.

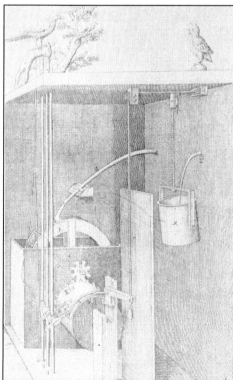

Figure 3. Explanatory illustration of a singing bird automataton; From Salomon de Caus, *Von gewaltsamen Bewegungen* (1615), Book I.

Informal Garden Design and the Idea of Wilderness

The concept of wilderness was part of formal as well as informal design styles. The term "wilderness" is defined in *A Glossary of Garden History* for both types of gardens:

> Basically a designed grove or wood with paths cut through it.... The essence of a wilderness is that it is ornamental, an attractive area in which to wander or pause. In formal gardens it was laid out at some distance from the house, beyond the parterre. The shape of the grove was usually regular though the design within it could be varied. Trees were generally laid out in rows.... Later on, in the more naturalistic landscapes of the eighteenth and early nineteenth centuries, a wilderness would be an informal woodland area of mixed species.[14]

With the decline of formal garden design and the stylistic shift from formal to landscape garden, wilderness and wild nature remained components of the concept of garden art. But over time there arose, perhaps as a consequence of the increasing interconnection between garden and landscape, a growing desire to turn the whole countryside, and with it nature and wilderness, into a garden.

In his book *Landscape and Memory*, Simon Schama offers his ideas on how wilderness found its way into the landscape garden, a wilderness that represented a "very polite kind of rudeness":

> A succession of remarkable landscape gardening books, beginning in 1700 with Timothy Nourse's *Campania Foelix* and continuing with Stephen Switzer's *Ichnographia Rustica* and Batty Langley's *New Principles of Gardening*, all extolled the virtues of what were designated as 'rude wilderness.' But when they were actually created, like the 'Elysium' at Castle Howard, featuring a sixty-acre forest dotted with Ionic temples, it was the Virgilian, rather than the archaic idea of arcadia that the gardeners had firmly in mind. It was wilderness, up to a point, the sort of thing seen in paintings by Claude and Poussin.... So when the fences and walls that had closed off formal gardens from the rural estate were removed, the unbroken view enjoyed by the magnate was a very polite kind of rudeness.[15]

The idea of representing wilderness in garden art seems to have lost much of its appeal in Europe during the nineteenth century. Perhaps the longing for nature and wilderness and the inclusion of wilderness in the Western world of experience was increasingly satisfied by other means such as the expeditions by Alexander von Humboldt, Georg Forster, and others. These explorers traversed other continents, discovered regions hitherto unknown to the Western world, and made them accessible to Western culture through literary descriptions and drawings. In light of these descriptions of genuine wildernesses, it was to be expected that artificial wildernesses in European garden art lost their authenticity and powers of persuasion.

In the evolution of the landscape garden in Germany, we can point to an increasing desire to take design ambitions beyond the garden and the surrounding landscape and to apply aesthetic criteria and aesthetic treatment to entire

Figure 4. Wörlitz (1998): the park blends into the agricultural landscape.

regions. This trend began in England with the idea of the ornamented farm. In Germany, the concept of *Landesverschönerung* (beautification of the land) appeared in the early nineteenth century. The *Dessau-Wörlitzer Gartenreich* (Dessau-Wörlitz garden empire) of Prince Leopold Friedrich Franz of Anhalt-Dessau (1740-1817) is probably the earliest German example of turning an entire region into a garden [Figure 4]. Although the Wörlitz park still incorporated elements of wilderness, Prince Leopold's ambitions were primarily directed toward eliminating any remnants of wilderness. He pursued this aim through the transformation of uncultivated and neglected landscapes into the *Gartenreich* as well as through educating his subjects according to humanistic precepts based on both his aesthetic and economic expectations. From the *Landesverschönerungsbewegung* (land beautification movement) sprang the idea of "Germany, all of Germany as a vast garden," as Jonathan Schuderoff put it in his pamphlet *Für Landesverschönerung* (1825). Over time, this idea gained broad currency.[16]

William Robinson's "Wild Garden" and Willy Lange's "Naturgarten"

Socio-economic developments gave renewed impetus to the notion of taking wilderness and nature as an ideal for garden design during the nineteenth century. This ideal was articulated in the English "wild garden" and the German *Naturgarten*.[17] England again played a leading role, as it had with the invention of the landscape garden. The reasons for the emergence of the wild garden and the *Naturgarten* are manifold: industrialization, urban expansion, railway construction, the transformation of agricultural and forest landscapes into areas for housing, industry, and commerce. All of these developments brought about harmful environmental conditions as a result, for example, of increased air and water pollution. More and more of what could be called "wild" nature in England and Germany was destroyed. The home protection movement (*Heimatschutzbewegung*) and the nature preservation movement, the successors to the land embellishment movement, consequently sought to turn entire regions, including wilderness and devastated areas, into landscapes that were at once aesthetically pleasing, ecologically sound, and economically productive.

It was the Irish garden writer William Robinson (1838-1935) who presented ideas about the wild garden in numerous books and articles, beginning with his book *The Wild Garden* [Figure 5]. Robinson's publications were widely read and influential in Europe, America, and other continents. In Germany, it was the garden architect and writer Willy Lange (1864-1941) who developed and propagated the concept of the *Naturgarten*—thirty years after Robinson's seminal book—in a series of articles in the magazine *Die Gartenwelt* [figure 6].[18] Lange, who had read Robinson, was highly influential in Germany and Scandinavia, and through the American garden architect Frank A. Waugh he had an impact in the United States as well.

Figure 5. The "wild garden": Gravety, the home of William Robinson. From Wilhelm Miller, *What England Can Teach Us About Gardening* (Garden City, NY, 1911).

The era in which Robinson published his garden theory saw the "second phase of industrialization."[19] Economic development was no longer based on the expansion of the textile industry but rather on the expansion of heavy industry. Even though it began several decades later, the process of industrialization moved as quickly in Germany as in England. During this period (1840-95), the German nature preservationist Ernst Rudorff railed against the unnatural, dangerous and monstrous growth of the cities.[20] Robinson criticized the results of industrialization in similar terms in his book *The English Flower Garden* (1883): "To-day the

Figure 6. Willy Lange's garden in springtime. From Willy Lange, *Gartengestaltung der Neuzeit* (1909).

ever-growing city, pushing its hard face over our once beautiful land, should make us wish more and more to keep such beauty of the earth as may still be possible to us; and the railway embankments, where once were the beautiful suburbs of London, cry to us to save all we can of the natural beauty of the earth." [21]

Let me note in passing that the different social groups in England and Germany experienced the effects of these changes in different ways. Members of the proletariat were not concerned with garden art. They were preoccupied with trying to improve their basic living conditions: with reducing working hours, abolishing child labor, and similar concerns. For them, garden culture could only mean production of food and enjoyment of space and air. Their needs are reflected in the growth of a strong allotment holders movement (*Kleingartenbewegung*). The longing for wilderness, the search for the wild or the natural garden, held no attraction for them.

Garden art developed as an interest of the upper middle class. Following victory in the war against France (1870-71) and the founding of the Reich (1871), industrialization and urbanization in Germany were given additional stimulation by the receipt of five billion francs in reparations from France. The members of Germany's new upper-middle class during this period of economic expansion were keen on possessing villa gardens and increasingly sought out specialists to design their gardens in the "ubiquitously emerging garden suburbs."[22]

Both Robinson and Lange developed their ideas on natural gardens at a time when the profession of garden architecture was still in its formative stage and was struggling for its very existence. The garden architects' main rivals were the architects, who had appropriated the field of garden design by replacing the ruling garden fashions in both countries. They supplanted earlier fashions with an all-embracing design and the application of homogeneous aesthetic principles to the design of the house, its rooms, and the garden. The garden itself was defined as an enlarged dwelling space; its design was primarily determined by owners' interests in outdoor activities. The formal garden was the architects' ideal.

German architect Hermann Muthesius articulated his ideas about the formal garden and the leading role of the architect in his book *Landhaus und Garten* in 1907:

> We must insist unconditionally on the fact that garden and house form a unit of which the main features must be thought out by the same genius. The relations between both are of such an intimate nature that it is absolutely impossible for two different persons, the architect and the gardener, strangers to each other, to design the house and its surroundings, as has been the case until now.... The corresponding aim in the case of the smaller house garden is to replace the landscape garden with the formal garden.[23]

Lange and Robinson developed their concepts of the nature garden and the wild garden not only as a reaction to the endangerment of nature by industrialization but also as a means to regain ground in the competition with architects. Designing natural or wild gardens required botanical and scientific knowledge on such topics as natural plant associations and their living conditions—knowledge that architects rarely possessed.

The seemingly self-contradictory terms "wild garden" and *Naturgarten* are anything but easy to define. It is possible, however, to identify common points in the thinking of Lange and Robinson as well as characteristic features in the work of their followers. Lange and Robinson oppose, for example, geometrical and architectonic forms; theirs is an informal garden style. A garden exists, in their view, not primarily to serve human beings, but rather to state that nature has equal rights, that plants and animals have equal rights. "Native" plants are to be preferred to "foreign" ones. Moreover, the garden is interpreted as a part of the surrounding landscape and is thus to be subordinated to it. The ideal nature garden does not require the care of a gardener; indeed, such care is to be avoided. For example, leaves should not be removed but should remain on the ground to provide habitats for plants and animals. Pruning trees and shrubs is rejected as anthropocentric, an expression of human rule over nature. Wild nature should serve as a model, Lange in particular stressed. He published a series of articles beginning in 1900 in which he discussed how wild nature could serve as a model for the garden architect. In one on water and landscape, he presented fascinating photographs of natural waterfalls in German landscapes as inspiration for garden designs and pointed out their characteristics in order to enable the correct application of such models in the garden. [Figure 7][24]

Figure 7. Natural waterfall given as an example by Willy Lange in an article on water in the landscape. From *Die Garten Welt* (1901)

The term *Naturgarten* was not coined by Lange. It had been used much earlier by other authors. Wilhelm Neubert, for example, described the English influence on the development of German garden design in 1853 with the comment: "The term 'English garden' is properly applied to real nature gardens."[25] Thirty years earlier, Cranz, one of the founding members of the Verein zur Beförderung des Gartenbaues in den Königlich Preußischen Staaten published his ideas on how "to convert the sand desert [in regions of Prussia] into a nature garden."[26] For Cranz, the nature garden meant not the depiction of wilderness but, to the contrary, the elimination of wilderness and uncultivated landscape and the transformation of whole regions into gardens – the whole of nature as a garden.

Robinson's wild garden and Lange's *Naturgarten* were not really pleas for wilderness in the garden. Robinson used the term wild garden for the transition zone between the formally designed parts of the garden around the country house and the surrounding landscape. This particular zone was to be developed into a natural-looking garden landscape by using native plants or hardy foreign plants. One of Robinson's most popular motifs for the wild garden was the planting of thousands of narcissi, crocuses, and other flowers to create spectacular, colorful effects in meadows and at the edges of woods during springtime. It should be mentioned that creating this motif often resulted in the destruction of nature and wilderness because thousands of plants were taken from those parts of the landscape where they were still growing wild.

Lange's concept of the *Naturgarten* was strongly influenced by science and Darwinist thought, though not necessarily by what Darwin had actually written. The rapid progress of science in the second half of the nineteenth century was an international phenomenon that assumed a specifically national form in Germany. Darwin's *The Origin of Species* received particular attention in Germany; the theory of evolution was applied not only to natural but also to social phenomena there, and it gained considerable ideological influence. The principles of the survival of the fittest and of natural selection became fundamental tenets of *volkisch*-nationalistic ideology and were transferred to all spheres of social life. In 1913, Lange described the impact of scientific progress on garden design in his book *Der Garten und seine Bepflanzung*:

> Today we have a natural science that is based on the history of development. It teaches us, as far as the interrelations between creatures with their homeland and their fellow creatures are concerned, to understand the laws of life. Biology supersedes all previous knowledge, which was only superficial. Biology, applied to art, establishes a new, a biological aesthetic.[27]

This "biological aesthetic," however modern in its scientific inspiration, was socially reactionary, and it promoted dubious ideas about an assumed relationship between the German people and nature.

Lange was strongly influenced by the ideas of the German scientist Ernst Haeckel and adopted the term "ecology," which Haeckel was the first to use, from him. Lange was particularly impressed by Haeckel's criticism of the Christian concept of man as ruler over nature. Consequently, Lange argued against the "anthropocentric" world view of the Old Testament, which placed man at the center of things:

> Perhaps we owe to the Old Testament the human right of dominion over creatures in an arbitrary way: to arrange various plants artificially in the garden, to water them here, to feed them there and to shut them up in the borders of the beds. This corresponds to the human sense of orderliness and to the right to rule, which has been preached for thousands of years.[28]

In Lange's view, plants should be granted equal rights: "On the basis of this world view we give the same right to plants to enjoy life as we do to ourselves."[29] The *Naturgarten* was his (garden) architectural and ethical response.

An essential aspect of Lange's idea of the *Naturgarten* was the conviction that the German people were deeply rooted in the soil, especially in the landscapes where they were born and lived. He concluded that every German required and deserved an appropriately designed environment. The subordination of the garden to the landscape and the use of "indigenous" plants became essential criteria for his natural garden design. Lange wrote:

> Our feelings for our homeland should be rooted in the character of the domestic landscapes; therefore it is German nature that must provide all the ideas for the design of gardens. They can be heightened by artistic means, but we must not give up the German

physiognomy. Thus, our gardens become German if the ideas for the design are German, especially if they are borrowed from the landscape in which the garden is situated.[30]

Surprisingly, Lange's concept of *Naturgarten* design and its close relationship to the surrounding landscape allowed—like Robinson's wild garden—the use of so-called foreign plants. Plants considered characteristic of the local landscape could be planted alongside foreign plants as long as the foreign plants resembled the local ones physiognomically in order "to express the laws of life, the manifestation of the plant world in a deepened, characteristic way."[31]

Lange was one of the garden architects who prepared the ideological ground for National Socialism's influence on the field of garden design. He saw his *Naturgarten* as the highest evolutionary stage of garden art. According to Lange, the architectonic garden style expressed the anthropocentric and unnatural attitude of other cultures and of lower stages of cultural evolution. "The highest development of garden design is consequently based on the scientific *Weltanschauung* of our times and is reflected in the artistic nature garden."[32] In keeping with racist ideas about the superiority of the German people, this stage could only be reached by Germans. Lange saw the ability to implement the highest stage of garden art as a racial characteristic of the Germanic or Nordic people. He explained, for example, the contrast between the formal French and the informal English garden style as the result of "different *Weltanschauungen* and these again by the differences between the souls of the two races." In the formal garden, Lange maintained, the Nordic race "perished spiritually in the race-morass of the South."[33] In 1933, the year the National Socialists took power, he mocked the formal garden of the "transalpine race" as an attempt by this "un-Nordic race to weaken the Nordic race" and to strengthen international anti-German forces.[34]

Lange, like many Germans during the Imperial and Weimar periods, adhered to the idea of the superiority of the German people that would become state doctrine under National Socialism. The following quotation exemplifies his understanding of cultural development as an evolutionary process:

> History will call this new stage of garden style, which is firmly based on its precursors, the stage of the German garden style. Germany has been chosen to lend its name to this style in the history of gardens and to become once again 'an enricher [*Veredler*] of the world.'[35]

Lange's case for the *Naturgarten* as the highest form of garden art was perhaps taken from art historians and art theorists such as Alois Riegl who believed that the use of geometrical styles in architecture and other art forms was a sign of low cultural development. In his *Stilfragen*, Riegel writes:

> The geometrical style according to the highest laws of symmetry and rhythm is the most perfect one from the point of view of regularity. But in our value system it is the lowest one and the evolution of the arts has shown that this style was mostly characteristic of nations on a relatively low cultural level.[36]

Riegl clearly abandons scholarly description of different cultures in statements like this and offers instead a subjective evaluation. Lange and other garden architects also used subjective evaluations along these lines to justify their racist idea that the *Naturgarten* is characteristic of the so-called Nordic races and is of a higher cultural level than the formal garden. The concept of the *Naturgarten* thus had a close affinity with National Socialism's ideology of "blood and soil" and thereby gained particular ideological significance in Germany during the National Socialist period.

National Socialist Landscape Architecture: The Antithesis of Wilderness

German garden architects who supported the Nazi dictatorship developed their ideas into a Nazi doctrine of landscape design. The work of a planning team under the supervision of SS Reichsführer Heinrich Himmler during World War II in the conquered Polish territories, the "Annexed Eastern Areas" (*eingegliederte Ostgebiete*), is an outstanding example.[37] The basic goal of Himmler's planning team was to reshape large parts of Polish territory entirely as landscapes based on the German ideal.

Wilderness played an exclusively negative role in this context. The term was sometimes used derogatorily, in the sense of wasteland or devastated land, to prove that the inhabitants of those particular regions were "racially," that is, innately, incapable of designing "ecologically" proper landscapes. National Socialist landscape planners juxtaposed the landscapes of Poland—or more accurately, their negative perceptions of these landscapes—with the ideal of "all of Germany as a garden."

After the invasion of Poland, the Nazis divided the areas which fell to Germany as a result of the German-Soviet pact into the Annexed Eastern Areas and the so-called Generalgouvernement. The Annexed Eastern Areas were to be incorporated into the German Reich and settled by Germans after the war. The Generalgouvernement was intended to serve as a collecting area for people the Nazis had expelled from their homes in other regions.

Himmler established various planning authorities shortly after the attack on Poland in his capacity as Reichskommissar für die Festigung deutschen Volkstums (Reich Commissioner for the Strengthening of Germanism), including one for landscape planning. According to National Socialist ideology, the occupation of this territory was a political necessity for the German people. New living space was to be secured by annexation. The German farmers who were to be settled there, it was argued, needed the ideal German landscape so that they would feel at home in the new territories and be willing to defend them. German landscape planning was thus closely related to the annexation. Numerous planners and landscape architects took part in these activities under Himmler's supervision.

Himmler had been entrusted with the position of Reich Commissioner for the Strengthening of German Values in a secret decree Hitler issued on October 7, 1939. According to the decree, Himmler's responsibilities were:

1. The final repatriation of those German citizens and ethnic Germans who are eligible for permanent return to the Reich.
2. The elimination of the harmful influence of such alien parts of the people that constitute a danger to the Reich and the German community of people.
3. The formation of new German territories for resettlement, especially by those ethnic Germans returning from foreign countries.[38]

Himmler was particularly interested in the third of these tasks, the "formation of new German territories for resettlement" and the unprecedented challenge it presented. Himmler created a planning board within the Reich Commission for the Strengthening of German Values under the supervision of SS-Oberführer Konrad Meyer. Meyer had headed the Institute of Agriculture and Land Politics at the University of Berlin since 1934. Two other important members of Himmler's planning board were garden architect Heinrich Friedrich Wiekping-Jürgensmann and Erhard Mäding. Wiekping-Jürgensmann, who held the chair at the Institute for Landscape Design at the Landwirtschaftliche Hochschule Berlin from 1934 to 1945, was appointed Special Representative for questions of landscape formation by Himmler. Mäding was officer for landscape formation. Landscape formation was, according to Mäding, the "most important task at present":

> The work of landscape formation goes above and beyond physical and organic living conditions. Germans will be the first occidental people to form their own spiritual environment in the landscape and will thereby, for the first time in the history of mankind develop a way of life in which a people consciously determines the local conditions for its physical and mental well-being.[39]

Mäding's vision did not leave much room for wilderness. The task was to design not only the physical environment for the German people but also the spiritual environment. Realizing this vision was possible only under dictatorial conditions. The expulsion and extermination of the Polish population living in these regions was a prerequisite for Nazi landscape planning. That landscape planners in the Annexed Eastern Areas did not need to consider the rights of people living there is clearly illustrated by Meyer's definition of "true freedom for planning":

> It is an essential feature of true freedom for planning that 1. members of the German race are available in sufficient numbers and with appropriate qualifications to take possession of new space, and 2. that property that is not possessed by members of their own people [i.e., the Germans] be available to the extent necessary.[40]

As Meyer's statement makes clear, the expulsion of the Polish population was a fundamental planning factor. It is not true that the garden architects were ignorant of the prerequisites for their work during the National Socialist era, as they later claimed. Himmler's planners knew about them and even referred to them in an exhibition, most likely the exhibition *Planung und Aufbau im Osten* (Planning and Construction in the East) organized by Himmler's planning board.

The high-minded claim about creating a "spiritual environment" in the land-scape for the German people was formulated by Mäding, Meyer, and Wiepking-Jürgensmann. Together, they exhibited a turpitude unprecedented in the history of the garden architecture profession in Germany. Wiepking-Jürgensmann, for example, wrote:

> We want to preserve the German people with German landscapes and have to lead in addition, a large number of eligible others [*Volksgenossen*], even rural people, into a spiritual landscape that corresponds to our nature and our spirit. The human spirit can run wild and create patterns of thought [*Ausbildungen des Denkens*] whose effects we may want to disavow.[41]

When wilderness was mentioned at all, it carried negative connotations. It was used in reference to people in Eastern Europe who, Himmler's planners argued, were incapable of designing cultivated and aesthetically pleasing landscapes and would therefore have to live in deserted and wild landscapes. Wilderness thus stood for neglected and waste landscapes, not for wild and natural landscapes that, from the perspective of nature preservation, were valuable and worth preserving.[42]

Heinrich Wiepking played a leading role among Himmler's landscape planners and was responsible for creating a negative image of the Polish people. He took as his ideal a statement by Hitler that the whole of Germany should become a garden:

> When the goal of turning all of Germany into a vast garden was articulated already at the beginning of the nineteenth century and was even developed into a scientific system (Haushofer), then this goal has finally and totally been realized today, since the Führer in his most recent great speech promised the German working class to turn Germany into a garden.[43]

Mäding saw the objective of landscape planning as creating a *Gesamtraumkunst-werk*, an artwork encompassing the whole of an area: "Landscape design turns forest and fields and other useful areas [*Nutzflächen*] into a *Gesamtraumkunst-werk*. It creates the preconditions for the optimal use of such natural resources as soil, water, air, and light, and it aims at the development of a perfect community of plant life, animals and man in the German *Lebensraum*."[44]

Mäding juxtaposed this *Gesamtraumkunstwerk*, this "perfect community," with the purportedly apocalyptic landscapes of the Poles in the 1943 "Landscape Rules" drafted by the planning staff and signed by Himmler. These official regulations included recommendations and instructions for designing and developing the landscape in the conquered Polish territories. There were plans to codify the Landscape Rules after the war in a *Reichslandschaftsgesetz* (Reich Landscape Law). In his introduction to the Landscape Rules, Mäding wrote,

We are confronted here [in the annexed Polish territories] with extensive areas, often as far as the eye can see, of a devastated, plundered landscape [*Raublandschaft*] or desolate barren steppe, although according to plant classification the region still belongs to the domain of woodland. Swamps and flood areas lie side by side with parched areas. The humid western winds drive, without paying their dues, eastward …. The exploitation of mineral resources took place without regard to the community needs and to the undesigned and awful settlement areas, for example in Upper Silesia, where the sterile spoil heaps and mining areas, wreathed in vapors and gases, are interspersed with disgusting waters. One imagines one is in a horrible underworld landscape but not in a human habitat on earth. If German people are to feel at home in these spaces then they have to become German cultural landscapes. That requires, for the most part, a total redesign, if not a design from scratch.[45]

The contradictions between well-ordered, harmonious man-made landscapes and threatening wilderness or a landscape laid waste were sketched out cynically in *Der Untermensch,* a pamphlet edited by Reichsführer SS Heinrich Himmler. The people of the Soviet Union, this pamphlet declared, were incapable of coherent landscape design. The landscapes of Eastern Europe were described as the product of the actions of *Untermenschen,* of subhumans, and their ruling system:

For the human being alone is capable of putting a stamp on the landscape. Thus we see, on the one hand, Germany's ordered fertility, the harmonious layout of its fields, well-considered grouping of villages, and on the other hand the zone of impenetrable thickets, the steppe, the endless primeval forest through which silted-up rivers seek their turgid course. Poorly used fertile lap of the black earth, which could be a paradise, a European California, has in reality gone to seed, dreadfully neglected, to this day bearing the marks of a cultural disgrace without compare, an enduring accusation against the *Untermensch* and his rulers.[46]

Wiepking-Jürgensmann expressed similarly racist sentiments in his 1942 book *Die Landschaftsfibel* as he commented on the relationship between human beings and the landscape in which they live:

The landscape is always a form, an expression and a characteristic of the people living within it. It can be the gentle countenance of its spirit and soul, just as it can be the grimace of its soullessness [*Ungeist*] and of human and spiritual depravity. In any case, it is the infallible, distinctive mark of what a people feels, thinks, creates, and acts. It shows, with inexorable severity, whether a people is constructive and a part of the divine creative power or whether destructive forces must be ascribed to it. Therefore the German landscapes differ in all ways from those of the Poles and the Russians—just as the peoples themselves. The murders and atrocities of the Eastern peoples are engraved, as if by sharp razor, into the grimaces of their native landscapes.[47]

No further quotations are needed to document the Nazis' contempt for the lands of occupied Polish and Russian areas; they saw these regions as wilderness, the antithesis to their idealized view of Germany as one vast garden.

Wilderness, be it as threat or ideal, has often been of relevance in the history of garden design. Medieval garden culture saw the garden as needing to be protected from nature and wilderness by walls, fences, or hedges. The *hortus conclusus*, the enclosed garden, expressed this understanding of the relation between humankind, nature, and wilderness. With the Renaissance, nature and wilderness increasingly became subjects of garden art. Scientific progress and technological development produced artistic representation of wilderness in the garden. In the centuries that followed, representation of wilderness in the garden served to satisfy a longing for nature amid the continued human appropriation of nature through agriculture, settlements, and industrialization.

In response to the changes in natural landscapes and disappearance of wilderness that resulted from industrialization, garden architects in Germany, England, and elsewhere began to develop sophisticated concepts of natural and wild gardens in the late nineteenth century. In Germany, these concepts were shaped not only by ideas about nature but also by *völkisch* notions of the Germans' close relationship to their natural environment as represented in landscapes. This ideology had fatal implications for other nations during the era of National Socialism. Nazi landscape planners developed plans for turning the land robbed from Poland into ideal German landscapes in preparation for the Germans who would be settled there after the war. The expulsion of the Poles was seen as a prerequisite for the realization of Nazi plans for landscape design and environmental protection. In this context, German garden architects and landscape planners referred to wilderness in derogatory terms, calling it an expression of the "racial" incapacity of the Poles and Russians for coherent landscape design.

This aspect of the history of garden and landscape design in Germany, the proximity of professional ideas about nature and landscape to Nazi ideology, has been ignored for decades. It is up to future historical researchers to determine whether these dubious ideas about nature and wilderness disappeared along with National Socialism or if they survived or influenced professional ideas in the field of landscape architecture in Germany after 1945.

Notes

I would like to thank Christof Mauch for his stimulating and helpful comments, David Lazar for his editorial efforts, and Mic Hale for his help with the translation.

1. Max Oelschlaeger, *The Ideal of Wilderness: From Prehistory to the Age of Ecology* (New Haven, 1991); Simon Schama, *Landscape and Memory* (New York, 1995); Bayerische Akademie für Naturschutz und Landschaftspflege, *Schön wild sollte es sein ... "Wertschätzung und ökonomische Bedeutung von Wildnis* (Laufen/Salzach, 1999). The German translation of Schama's book is entitled *Der Traum von der Wildnis* —"The Dream of Wilderness." One can only speculate whether these different titles are indicative of differences between German and American readers' ideas about nature and wilderness.

2. *Chambers Twentieth-Century Dictionary* (1983 ed.), s.v. "wilderness."

3. Ibid.

4. On garden culture in the Middle Ages, see Dieter Hennebo, *Die Gärten des Mittelalters* (Munich, 1987).

5. See, for example, the discussion of Petrarch's perception of landscape in Joachim Ritter, "Landschaft. Zur Funktion des Ästhetischen in der modernen Gesellschaft," in Gert Gröning and Ulfert Herlyn, eds., *Landschaftswahrnehmung und Landschaftserfahrung*, Arbeiten zur sozialwissenschaftlich orientierten Freiraumplanung, vol. 10, second edition (Münster, 1996), 29-68.

6. Oelschlaeger, *The Idea of Wilderness*, 70.

7. Ibid., 72.

8. Ibid., 68.

9. Claudia Lazzaro, *The Italian Renaissance Garden: From the Conventions of Planting, Design, and Ornament to the Grand Gardens of Sixteenth-Century Central Italy* (New Haven: 1990), 8.

10. Ibid., 9.

11. John Dixon Hunt, *Greater Perfections: The Practice of Garden Theory* (Philadelphia, 2000), 32.

12. Lazzaro, *The Italian Renaissance Garden*, 9.

13. One of the most fascinating treatises expounding the idea of the garden as a representation of the world is the unfinished *Elysium Britannicum* by the seventeenth-century virtuoso John Evelyn: *Elysium Britannicum or the Royal Gardens*, John E. Ingram, ed. (Philadelphia, 2001). On Evelyn, see Therese O'Malley and Joachim Wolschke-Bulmahn, eds., *John Evelyn's "Elysium Britannicum" and European Gardening*, Dumbarton Oaks Colloquium on the History of Landscape Architecture, vol. 17 (Washington, D.C., 1998).

14. Michael Symes, *A Glossary of Garden History* (Princes Risborough, 1993) , 132f. *The Oxford Companion to Gardens* notes that in late seventeenth- and early eighteenth-century Europe "wilderness" was "the most common name to designate a wooded feature with (usually winding) paths running through it. This version of the bosquet developed while the formal garden still held sway . . . and the early exemplars were formal in many respects. In England the 17th-c. prototype, Wren's wilderness at Hampton Court, planted in 1689 by London and Wise, was geometrical in design with allées, based on two principal vistas, intersecting to form a St. Andrew's cross." Patrick Goode and Michael. Lancaster, eds., Sir Geoffrey Jellicoe and Susan Jellicoe, consulting editors, *The Oxford Companion to Gardens* (Oxford, 1986), 603ff.

15. Schama, *Landscape and Memory*, 538f.

16. Cf. Gert Gröning, "Anmerkung Zu Gustav Vorherrs Idee der Landesverschönerung," in Günter Bayerl, Norman Fuchsloch, and Torsten Meyer, eds., *Umweltgeschichte-Methoden, Themen, Potentiale* (Münster, 1996), 176.

17. On the wild garden and *Naturgarten*, see Joachim Wolschke-Bulmahn, "The 'Wild Garden' and the 'Nature Garden': Aspects of the Garden Ideology of William Robinson and Willy Lange," *Journal of Garden History* 12, no. 3 (1992): 183-206.

18. On Willy Lange, see Joachim Wolschke-Bulmahn and Gert Gröning, "Der kommende Garten. Zur Diskussion über die Gartenarchitektur in Deutschland seit 1900," *Garten und Landschaft* 98, no. 3 (1988): 47-56; Joachim Wolschke-Bulmahn and Gert Gröning, "From Open-Mindedness to Naturalism: Garden Design and Ideology in Germany During the Early Twentieth Century," *Journal of Home & Consumer Horticulture* 1 (1994): 133-51.

19. Eric J. Hobsbawm, *Industry and Empire: From 1750 to the Present Day,* The Pelican Economic History of Britain, vol. 3 (Harmondsworth, 1969).

20. Ernst Rudorff, "Ueber das Verhältniß des modernen Lebens zur Natur," *Preußische Jahrbücher* 45 (1880): 270.

21. William Robinson, *The English Flower Garden and Home Grounds*, eighth edition (London, 1900), 22.

22. Dieter Hennebo, "Gartenkünstler - Gartenarchitekt – Landschaftsarchitekt," in Bund Deutscher Landschafts-Architekten, ed., *Das Berufsbild des Garten- und Landschaftsarchitekten*, (Munich, 1973), 9.

23. Hermann Muthesius, *Landhaus und Garten. Beispiele neuzeitlicher Landhäuser nebst Grundrissen, Innenräumen und Gärten* (Munich, 1970), xxv.

24. Willy Lange, "Wasser in der Landschaft," *Die Gartenwelt* (1901): 115.

25. Wilhelm Neubert, ed., *Schlüssel zur bildenden Gartenkunst. Eine Anleitung zur Anlegung und Verschönerung von Gärten verschiedener Größe für Gärtner und Privatliebhaber* (Stuttgart, 1853).

26. Cranz, quoted in Gert Gröning, "The Idea of Land Embellishment as Exemplified in the *Monatsheft für Verbesserung des Landbauwesens und für zweckmäßige Verschönerung des baierischen Landes*," *Journal of Garden History* 12, no. 3 (1992): 173. And even earlier, in 1803, Christian August Semler used the term *Naturgarten* in his book *Ideen zu einer Gartenlogik*; see Gert Gröning, "Ideological Aspects of Nature Garden Concepts in Late Twentieth-Century Germany," Joachim Wolschke-Bulmahn, ed., *Nature and Ideology. Natural Garden Design in the Twentieth Century*, Dumbarton Oaks Colloquium on the History of Landscape Architecture, vol. 18 (Washington, D.C., 1997), 239, 244f.

27. Willy Lange, *Der Garten und seine Bepflanzung* (Stuttgart, 1913), 29.

28. Ibid., 14.

29. Willy Lange, "Gartengedanken," *Die Gartenkunst* 5 (1903): 100.

30. Willy Lange, *Gartengestaltung der Neuzeit* (Leipzig, 1907), 358.

31. Lange, *Der Garten und seine Bepflanzung*, 136.

32. Willy Lange, "Meine Anschauungen über die Gartengestaltung unserer Zeit," *Die Gartenkunst* 7 (1905): 114.

33. Willy Lange, *Gartenpläne* (Leipzig, 1927), 5.

34. Willy Lange, "Deutsche Gartenkunst," *Deutsche Kultur-Wacht* 2 (1933): 8.

35. Willy Lange, *Gartenbilder* (Leipzig, 1922), 27.

36. Alois Riegl, quoted in Wilhelm Worringer, *Abstraktion und Einfühlung. Ein Beitrag zur Stilpsychologie*, 8th edition (Munich, 1919), 22.

37. For more detail on landscape planning of Nazi Germany in the Annexed Eastern Areas, see Gert Gröning and Joachim Wolschke-Bulmahn, *Der Drang nach Osten. Zur Entwicklung der Landespflege im Nationalsozialismus und in den "eingegliederten Ostgebieten" während des Zweiten Weltkriegs*, Die Liebe zur Landschaft, part 2, Gert Gröning and Ulfert Herlyn, eds., Arbeiten zur sozialwissenschaftlich orientierten Freiraumplanung, vol. 9 (Munich, 1987).

38. Hitler-Erlaß 7. Oktokber 1939, Bundesarchiv Koblenz, R 49/2.

39. Erhard Mäding, *Landespflege. Die Gestaltung der Landschaft als Hoheitsrecht und Hoheitspflicht* (Berlin, 1942), 215f.

40. Konrad Meyer, *Reichsplanung und Raumordnung im Lichte der volkspolitischen Aufgabe des Ostaufbaus* (n. p., 1941), 12.

41. Heinrich Friedrich Wiepking-Jürgensmann, "Aufgaben und Ziele deutscher Landschaftspolitik," *Raumforschung und Raumordnung* 3, no. 7 (1939): 368.

42. The other use of the term "wilderness" can be found among National Socialist nature preservationists though not in the context of landscape planning activities under the supervision of Himmler in the annexed Eastern Areas.

43. Heinrich Friedrich Wiepking-Jürgensmann, "Ranmordnung und Landschaftsgestaltung. Um die Erhaltung der schöpferischen Kräfte des deutschen Volkes," *Ranmforschung und Ranmordnung* 5 (1941: 1,23.

44. Erhard Mäding, "Landespflege," *Reich, Volksordnung, Lebensraum. Zeitschrift für völkische Verfassung und Verwaltung* 3 (1942): 343.

45. Erhard Mäding, *Regeln für die Gestaltung der Landschaft. Einführung in die Allgemeine Anordunung Nr. 20/VI/42 des Reichsführers SS, Reichskommissars für die Festigung deutschen Volkstums, über die Gestaltung der Landschaft in den eingegliederten Ostgebieten* (Berlin, 1943), 14.

46. Reichsführer SS, ed. *Der Untermensch* (Berlin, 1942), 27.

47. Heinrich Friedrich Wiepking-Jürgensmann, *Die Landschaftsfibel* (Berlin, 1942), 13.

Chapter 5

FOR NATION AND PROSPERITY, HEALTH AND A GREEN ENVIRONMENT
Protecting Nature in West Germany, 1945-70

Sandra Chaney

Between 1945 and 1970, West Germany recovered from the devastation of total war and quickly emerged as a highly industrialized, affluent, urban nation that was the seventh most densely populated country in the world. Over this quarter century, nature underwent significant transformation, and so, too, did rationales for protecting it. In the first postwar decade, the cause of protecting nature, *Naturschutz,* generated limited concern because it seemed to stand in the way of economic recovery and industrial expansion. As rapid development brought about discernable ecological changes, however, West Germans were forced to alter their understanding of the natural world and why it ought to be protected. By the late 1960s and early 1970s, *Naturschutz* acquired a much broader base of popular support, largely because it had come to be seen as a small, but significant part of protecting human beings in their threatened environment, *Umweltschutz.*

Using the shift in emphasis from *Naturschutz* to *Umweltschutz* as a broad framework, this essay examines continuities and change in the dominant meanings assigned to nature in West Germany. The task is a worthwhile endeavor, for, as one scholar has written, "It seems unlikely that we can hope to 'save nature' without first ascertaining just what it is we think we are attempting to save."[1] But discerning general social attitudes about nature is a difficult task because, for much of the period, most West Germans were not engaged in activities or debates explicitly aimed at conservation. Thus, this brief study focuses primarily on the groups and individuals most intimately involved in protecting nature, examining how they justified their efforts, not only in terms of perceived threats to, and greater knowledge of, the natural world, but also in response to larger social, economic, and political concerns.

The essay begins with an exploration of the meanings associated with nature from 1945 until West Germany gained full sovereignty in 1955, a time when the exploitation of natural resources seemed essential to address the overriding concern for economic recovery. In these years, conservationists insisted that the careful planned use of natural resources was fundamental to economic revival. Protecting nature meant ensuring the country's economic future, for only with adequate natural resources could West Germany recover its economic vitality. This period also was marked by the persistence of traditional justifications for safeguarding nature in the form of natural monuments, nature reserves, and scenic landscapes that had been shaped by cultural traditions and that reflected unique regional, but especially national, heritages. In several instances, nature was conflated with *Heimat* (homeland), which seemed to demand protection against Allied or foreign exploitation. Forests, rivers, and cultural landscapes, for example, were imbued with national significance; protecting these seemingly "unsullied" natural features provided a way to assert a sense of national identity. By the 1950s, however, conservationists were more concerned about protecting nature from unbridled economic development, and in doing so asserted an alternative vision of a Germany that was not only materially wealthy, but also rich in natural beauty.

The years between 1955 and the late 1960s were marked by economic prosperity on the one hand, but also, on the other, worsening pollution and the overconsumption of fertile land to support the expansion of industry, transportation, and housing. During this period, nature continued to be valued as a resource for continued economic production, but was rarely associated with national identity. As nature registered the impact of rapid, intensified economic and technological development, conservationists argued that its protection was vital to public health and well-being. They gave their cause greater social relevance and widened public interest in a diluted version of *Naturschutz* by setting aside scenic rural landscapes to serve as nature parks where people could recuperate from what they described as the "unnatural" human-crafted urban environment. With more and more West Germans living in cities, nature assumed added importance as something that could be consumed in the form of recreation areas to enhance the quality of life. Heightened concern about the denatured everyday urban environment, however, broadened the scope of *Naturschutz* to include the construction of a more natural built environment, particularly in cities. Conservationists worked to protect and restore nature in country and city, in the local environment (which previously had been called *Heimat*) and in the nation. By the early 1970s, the protection of nature had been elevated to a higher level of importance, but only as a small part of the much more daunting challenge of safeguarding the human environment—protecting it at home, in the nation, and around the world.

After World War II, famine, population dislocation, shortages of natural resources, soil erosion, sinking water tables, and desertification across the world prompted neo-Malthusian warnings in the West about the need for human society to understand and conform to nature's limits.[2] In the western zones of Germany, these conditions seemed to be magnified. Territorial losses, the sudden influx of over ten million refugees and displaced persons, the challenge of feeding, housing, and ensuring fuel for a larger population in a smaller area after total economic and political collapse placed unprecedented demands on nature. As a leading conservationist in the war-torn province of Hanover wrote matter-of-factly in December 1945, "the loss of living space, the loss of numerous branches of production, and the end of participation in international trade and commerce will force us to exploit all possibilities of the local landscape."[3] More than ever before, he concluded, Germans would be forced to intensively farm, garden, and mine the land they still possessed, while simultaneously ensuring that it remained fertile and productive for long-term use.[4]

Failed harvests, forest fires, and abnormal summer and winter temperatures that marked the late 1940s provided ample evidence of past abuses of the land and posed serious challenges for the immediate future. Echoing fears expressed during the Third Reich about the deterioration of fertile land into exhausted steppe (*Versteppung*), individuals involved in state-sponsored conservation and recently revived private organizations asserted a more active approach to protecting nature. As they had attempted to do since the 1920s and 30s, conservationists argued that their work included not only narrow nature preservation, but also protecting, and in some cases restoring, the productivity of the land.

To express the expanded dimensions of their work they consistently paired the familiar concept *Naturschutz* with the term *Landschaftspflege*, meaning care of the landscape. The idea of "landscape" and its role in shaping Germany's conservation efforts is too complex to explore in any detail here.[5] It is critical to point out, however, that with no wilderness to speak of, conservationists in Germany long had understood that the nature they were interested in protecting had been shaped by centuries of human use. The concept "landscape" referred to nature that bore the mark of human culture but was hardly value-neutral for it conveyed a variety of aesthetic assumptions about nature and what it ought to look like. For example, scholars of the *Heimatschutz* movement argue that efforts to protect cultural landscapes in the late nineteenth- and early twentieth centuries conveyed ecological insight by envisioning a harmonious integration of natural features, cultural and architectural traditions, *and* economic development and modernization.[6] But it is clear that the aesthetic preferences of the movement's leaders and membership were reflected in these initiatives. The same cultural traditions that inspired turn-of-the-century landscape protection also assumed that the character of a people was reflected in the appearance of the land. By the 1920s and 1930s, this presumed organic link between landscapes and national character acquired racial overtones in preservationist discourse. Under National Socialism, such assumptions about nature and people guided landscape architects in trying to "Germanize" conquered eastern territories, supporting the forced removal of "racially inferior" local inhabitants who supposedly degraded the landscape.[7]

After the war racialized definitions of "landscape" disappeared, but nationalistic understandings persisted in some circles well into the 1950s. The concept "landscape" continued to convey biased conceptions of nature, but acquired an additional layer of meaning that gave it weight in scientific discourse. As one prominent conservationist explained in the 1960s, "landscape" referred to a part of the earth's surface that was a tangible unit, not only because of its visible vegetation and terrain, but also because of less apparent factors such as climate and surface and ground water. It was the work of conservationists to ensure that landscapes, both rural and urban, remained or were restored to a healthy condition.[8] This attempt to define landscape in terms of its "real" qualities revealed the broader scope of conservation, which aimed to protect not only flora and fauna, natural monuments, or scenic parts of the countryside, but also to revitalize spaces in rural and urban areas.

Until the 1960s, however, the legal and administrative foundations for conservation in West Germany proved inadequate to address this broader agenda. During the occupation, the Reich Conservation Law (*Reichsnaturschutzgesetz*, RNG) of 1935 was purged of "authoritarian elements" by occupation authorities,[9] and its provisions were eventually subsumed within state, not federal, law under the Federal Republic.[10] When passed in 1935, the RNG had marked the culmination of efforts since the 1920s to pass national conservation legislation, and was progressive in its provisions to preserve plants, animals, reserves, and natural monuments. But the law did little to protect large areas of land or to rehabilitate spaces damaged by development, responsibilities that assumed greater importance after the war.[11]

West German states also inherited the administrative organization for conservation that had been set forth in the RNG. Under the federal structure, however, the highest conservation office no longer resided at the national level, but in state ministries of culture, agriculture, or the interior.[12] To aid conservation officials who often lacked the expertise and time to address conservation adequately, the RNG had built on an earlier tradition by creating independent agencies (*Naturschutzstellen*) headed by honorary commissioners (*Beauftragter*) who were drawn largely from the ranks of the professional middle classes.[13] Until the late 1960s, some commissioners at the state level, and most at the district and county levels, were volunteers, performing their duties with little financial support and in addition to their occupations (often as biology teacher, forester, landscape architect, or engineer).[14] These commissioners cooperated closely with the Federal Institute for Conservation (*Bundesanstalt für Naturschutz und Landschaftspflege*, BANL), an establishment with a tradition dating back to the early twentieth century.[15] Through the tireless efforts of Hans Klose, the agency's director since 1939, the institute survived postwar austerity measures to chart the course of official conservation in West Germany. Klose also hoped to maintain uniformity in state-sponsored conservation through the Working Association of German Commissioners for Conservation (*Arbeitsgemeinschaft Deutscher Beauftragter für Naturschutz und Landschaftspflege*), a professional organization he founded in 1947. The institute and commissioners labored to convince officials and a public understandably more concerned with regaining economic stability that the protection of nature was not merely a cultural endeavor to preserve natural monuments (such as unique geological formations, groves of old trees, or waterfalls) or nature reserves for scientific research or aesthetic enjoyment. Rather, conservation included maintaining the long-term productivity of landscapes and natural resources (*Landschaftspflege*).[16]

By promoting *Naturschutz* and *Landschaftspflege* as two complementary aspects of the broader effort to protect and conserve nature, conservationists asserted that they had a vital role to play in economic revival. Only planning and guiding the use of soil, water, forests, and minerals would ensure that the land remained healthy enough to support intensified agricultural production and postwar reconstruction in the present and industrial expansion in the years ahead.[17] With such arguments, conservationists expressed hope in the organic renewal of a Germany that once again would be economically productive.

Conservationists also assumed, however, that they were helping to rebuild a *Heimat*, a place where people would once again feel at home in the comfort of familiar customs and traditions and beautiful natural surroundings. At a time when Germans were working to rebuild shattered communities, some conservationists asserted, nature provided temporary refuge from the want and worry of the present. In nature, people could find spiritual strength for clearing away the rubble in the cities and in their souls.[18] Those rural areas in the western zones that had managed to escape the ravages of war seemed to have remained untainted by the recent past and potentially served as sites for national renewal.

Particularly while defending nature that was under attack, however, conservationists, and political leaders who supported their goals, expressed a green nationalism that reaffirmed ties to the past and asserted a positive national identity. This is illustrated vividly in the debate surrounding allied treatment of forested land in the western zones. In 1946, the United States Office of Military Government announced plans for "full exploitation" of German forests during the first two years of the occupation.[19] Later that year, the British began "Operation Woodpecker," dispatching three thousand soldiers armed with axes to fell trees in the Harz Mountains and the Lüneburg Heath.[20] Timber was urgently needed to rebuild homes, restore transportation lines, construct pit props for mining, and—with coal production low—to serve as a source of household fuel.[21] Furthermore, Germany's timber was exported to generate revenue to pay for essential goods that had to be imported, and to meet reparations obligations.[22] In this case, nature provided a powerful reminder of the recent past and reinforced the Germans' status as a defeated people.

In opposing the "dismantling" of forested areas, German political leaders claimed the status of victims of the Nazi regime as well as of the occupying powers. At the same time, however, they were able to engage in an act of protest that also demonstrated patriotism.[23] According to Bavaria's Minister of Agriculture, Dr. Josef Baumgartner (Bavaria Party) in 1947, "The slaughter of German forests

… the destruction of vast forested areas, and the exploitation of timber reserves that have been tended for decades" was a "catastrophe." The National Socialist regime had begun an "irresponsible exploitation" (*verantwortungsloser Raubbau*) of Germany's forests in 1934, he declared, and the Allied powers were continuing it at a rate that would disrupt the water supply and microclimate and would ultimately affect the economy of Germany and Europe adversely.[24] Baumgartner and other political leaders in Bizonia alleged that the extent of overcutting in the western zones violated the 1907 Hague Convention, which set limits on the amount of raw materials victors could extract from another country.[25] In explaining why such complaints went unheeded, a Braunschweig forester concluded that the occupying powers lacked the attachment to forests that Germans had cultivated over generations through sound forestry practices, as well as through sagas, poetry, and music that had been inspired by the woods.[26]

Frustrated by the slow response of the occupying powers, prominent members of the British Zonal Advisory Council initiated a "people's movement" of protest from above by establishing the Society for the Protection of the German Forest (*Schutzgemeinschaft Deutscher Wald*, or SDW) in December 1947. This reference to the many distinct regional forests as one unified German forest provided a way to express a desire for national unity that was rooted in nature and positive German traditions. In exhibits, publications, and lectures, SDW chapters emphasized the economic and ecological significance of well-tended forests, but also sought to remind Germans of what SDW literature described as an enduring cultural bond between forest and *Volk*. This imagined link with a better, distant past provided foundations for reconstructing a positive national identity. Particularly concerned about the younger generation, SDW enlisted girls and boys to help rebuild the country, encouraging them to reforest their *Heimat*.[27] This organic renewal was symbolically linked with the country's economic revival when West Germany designed its new currency; the 50 pfennig coin bore the imprint of a barefoot woman planting an oak seedling (a tree considered to be authentically German, despite being an importation).[28]

On the first SDW-sponsored "Day of the Tree" in April 1952 (modeled after Arbor Day in the U.S.), national chapter president Robert Lehr[29] sought to awaken a sense of national identity that was based on allegedly unique cultural ties to nature. "We Germans," he told participants in Bonn, "have always been connected to the forest in a … heartfelt way.… Painters, poets and musicians created enduring works that move us profoundly in times when we reflect on ourselves as a people and give us strength, clarity and faith." According to Lehr, "[c]ustoms, ways of thinking, character—yes, our soul is deeply anchored in the forest, in the *Heimat* of fairy tales and sagas."[30] When Chancellor Konrad Adenauer addressed the Berlin chapter of SDW in 1953, he announced that the German forest "is for us something that is deeply tied to the German essence. Whoever loves the German forest also loves an orderly political system. But he loves something more—he also loves the German *Heimat* out of the depths of [his] soul."[31]

In invoking the forest as a symbol of the German *Heimat,* Adenauer sought to awaken a sense of community in the nation. Celia Applegate has argued that *Heimat* was "[p]ulled out of the rubble of the Nazi Reich as a victim, not a perpetrator." *Heimat,* she maintains, "embod[ied] the political and social community that could be salvaged from the Nazi ruins." Though Applegate emphasizes how *Heimat* was used to reclaim "traditional provincialism" as Germans' primary identity after the war, some such as Adenauer and Lehr used the notion of an untainted *Heimat* to inspire a sense of national identity.[32] Despite such conservative rhetoric about the forest as a symbol of the German national *Heimat,* however, there is indication that Germans' tie to the forest might not have been so deeply anchored. According to a 1955 poll of approximately 2,000 people conducted by the Allensbach Institute, 55 percent responded they did not visit the forests often and another 11 percent indicated they had not been to the forests in years.[33]

Overtly nationalistic justifications for protecting nature became less frequent and more muted in discourse in the 1950s, but did not disappear, particularly when it seemed that nature and treasured scenic landscapes were threatened by foreign exploitation. To cite but one example, in June 1956 an estimated one thousand German students protested the continued presence of British military forces in their "national park," the Lüneburg Heath nature reserve. This protected area was located in the vast low-lying plain in north central Germany, which military theorists considered to be a likely site for a Soviet-launched attack. Though the British used the heath for military training less frequently after the Federal Republic gained full sovereignty and joined NATO in 1955, they continued to tear up parts of the reserve. During the evening of June 23, Herbert Wehner, a leading SPD deputy in the West German parliament, told students that their torches burned as a sign of peace and understanding among peoples. The Federal Republic was not a colony, he insisted; it asserted the right of self-determination. Area newspaper reports glorified the "declaration of the German youth for the liberation of the *Heimat*" and their appeal to "end once and for all the humiliation and destruction inflicted on us by foreign troops."[34]

In the process of protecting this cultural landscape, students, politicians, and journalists elevated the heath to the status of a "national park" (even though it hardly could be called one) or referred to it as a "colonial possession," a besieged *Heimat* that needed to be liberated from foreign exploitation. Protecting nature in this particular case also involved defending feelings of national pride and asserting West Germany's new status as fully sovereign nation. It is not entirely clear, however, if these protestors felt an attachment to the Federal Republic as a nation-state or to the idea of an autonomous German nation. Scholars who have examined the process of constructing national identity after 1945 explain that in the 1950s and 1960s few expressed firm ties to the Federal Republic, a political entity that was presumed to be temporary. It was more common for West Germans to convey a muted sense of pride in their country by focusing on its economic prosperity.[35]

From the perspective of conservationists, however, the country's rapid economic growth threatened to deprive West Germans of a part of their natural heritage and compromised the quality of air and water, and the health of the land. Beginning in the late 1940s, several new national conservation organizations, alliances, "protective associations," and "working associations" formed to educate the public about the need to protect nature. The German Conservation Ring (*Deutscher Naturschutzring*) (1950), an umbrella organization that soon united sixty-one member organizations representing 760,000 people, worked closely with state-sponsored conservation agencies and offices to protect threatened species, protest development projects, improve biology instruction in public schools, and elevate the status of honorary commissioners. Other new organizations concentrated on specific issues, such as forest or water conservation, wildlife preservation, or noise pollution.[36] In 1952, politicians' concern for protecting nature galvanized when fifty federal and state parliamentarians from diverse political parties formed the Interparliamentary Working Group for a Sustainable Economy (*Interparlamentarische Arbeitsgemeinschaft für eine naturgemässe Wirtschaft*) to promote conservation in tandem with economic development.[37]

Individuals associated with state-sponsored conservation as well as those involved in new and long-standing organizations asserted, as they had since the late nineteenth century, that protecting nature did not mean opposing "progress" unequivocally. By the 1950s, the economic growth they originally had supported seemed to know no bounds. Private organizations cooperated with conservation officials and honorary commissioners, the press, and state parliamentarians to halt plans to build more chairlifts on scenic mountains, prevent rivers from being exploited by utility companies, and protest the spread of weekend houses, some of them truly unsightly, in the open countryside. In objecting to these and other development projects that seemed unnecessary, conservationists acquired a reputation for being uncompromising, unreasonable, and overly sentimental. They responded that their actions to preserve natural monuments, plant and animal species, nature reserves, or treasured landscapes that bore the mark of centuries of human culture demonstrated moral restraint, respect for creation, and a commitment to future generations. Promoting conservation, they argued, expressed greater foresight and an appreciation for unquantifiable, non-material values in an era that otherwise seemed to be marked by materialism, an insatiable hunger for land, an obsession with technology, and the unrestrained pursuit of profit.[38]

When conservation commissioners and private organizations took action to protect treasured landscapes and reserves, such as the Wutach Gorge in Baden-Württemberg, the Upper Lech in Bavaria, or the Mosel Valley in Rhineland-Palatinate, they often erroneously referred to these landscapes as "original," "pristine," or even "primeval," implying perhaps that they represented sacred space that ought to be off limits to development. Though all of these areas were unique, they were hardly untouched. Such romanticized references to nature that seemed less sullied by economic projects and technology reflected a desire to preserve at least some landscapes of cultural significance from the homogenization that often accompanied unbridled development. But idealized descriptions of nature, readily dismissed by opponents, tended to obscure conservationists' arguments, which were actually quite complex. In their campaigns to protect nature, conservationists presented scientific research that underscored the necessity of fertile land, well-managed forests, and a reliable supply of clean water not only for economic growth, but also for general social well-being.[39] Nonetheless, conservationists' activities continued to be seen as protecting nature from people, not for them.

A specific example that illustrates the diverse rationales for protecting nature and the shifting emphasis away from defending *Heimat* or the nation to promoting public health and social welfare is the debate over the Mosel River and Valley. In 1956, Chancellor Adenauer agreed to France's demand to canalize the scenic Mosel River between Thionville and Koblenz as partial compensation for France's loss of the Saar to West Germany. Adenauer concluded that constructing the canal was a small price to pay for the return of the Saar and the continuation of talks on Western European integration. The majority of West Germans supported the chancellor's decision, including citizens in Rhineland-Palatinate who would be directly affected by the project.[40]

Vocal opposition came from Ruhr industrialists and the German Federal Railway, who feared increased competition (but expressed little concern about the Mosel River), and a less powerful group of West Germans in conservation, *Heimat,* and youth organizations, and scientific societies who anticipated the "destruction" of a beloved cultural landscape. Individuals one could loosely call conservationists sent several hundred letters and postcards to the chancellor and the Foreign Office in 1956, instructing Adenauer to not sacrifice this "jewel of the German *Heimat*"[41] to the economic interests of profit-seeking foreigners.[42] The State Fishery Association of Rhineland-Rhine-Hesse urged Adenauer to not make the Mosel a "chain of drainage basins for French industrial effluents." France's inadequate laws against water pollution, the association alleged, would do little to prevent businesses and industries in France from dumping effluents into the river.[43] They conveniently overlooked their own country's tainted rivers, which were the focus of increased state and federal attention.[44]

These letters conveyed a sense of national pride in claiming to defend the uniquely German Mosel River and Valley from the exploitative economic interests of a foreign nation.[45] But they also voiced resentment over France's continued influence on West German foreign policy and its ability, so it seemed, to determine the fate of a treasured part of Germany's natural heritage. Such anti-French sentiments are not altogether surprising: the debate concerned a river that flowed through territory that had long been contested between France and Germany. In 1956, however, some contended that a canalized Mosel River symbolized West Germany's tenuous status as a sovereign nation.

More frequently, correspondence viewed plans to canalize the Mosel as confirmation of their fears that West Germany was losing its scenic landscapes to urban and industrial sprawl at an alarming rate. Some lamented that so many beautiful landscapes already had been lost to housing developments or to technology in general, giving the impression that West Germans were excessively materialistic.[46] Others were more concerned that this popular recreation area and affordable vacation spot would be despoiled. A Duisburg engineer explained that for those who "spend the largest part of our lives in a gray environment" the Mosel "brings us not only good wine" but also "peaceful idyllic nature in which tense nerves can relax and the soul can gain new strength."[47] Some letter-writers emphasized that adding locks, dams, and concrete retaining walls would not only alter the appearance of this unique river and valley, but also would reduce the fish population and biological diversity of vegetation along the shores.[48] Though their appeals ultimately failed to halt the project, conservationists and concerned citizens reminded diplomats that the Mosel was not merely another transportation route. The valley was a popular tourist destination and a beautiful cultural landmark of intangible value to the region and nation, but also a living river that supported diverse plant and animal life and provided communities with drinking water that had to be kept clean.

By the late 1950s, convincing arguments for making conservation socially relevant required talking about the protection of nature less in terms of moral values and cultural traditions or its meaning for *Heimat* and nation, and more in terms of its relevance for public health, recreation, and regional planning. In the latter half of the 1950s, pressure to protect some of the Federal Republic's most scenic landscapes for the population increased because of growing concern about public health. By the early 1960s, an estimated 50 percent of West Germans lived in urban areas with forty thousand or more inhabitants, many of them enjoying significant improvements in their standard of living. Paradoxically, this prosperity was accompanied by what medical experts dubbed "diseases of civilization" or "manager illnesses"—higher instances of fatigue, high blood pressure, heart disease, and cancer—that were associated with living in an affluent, urban, industrial society. According to doctors, industrialists, conservationists, and a host of others, millions of West Germans had not adapted to the fast-paced urban society they had created and needed to recover from the stress of daily life by spending time in nature.[49]

Concern that city life threatened public health echoed an earlier critique of urban, industrial society that reflected ambivalence about modernity, but it also reflected a broader understanding of health beyond the absence of disease.[50] Higher expectations about health and well-being were indicative of an improved standard of living, but they also had developed in response to the tangible threats to public health posed by worsening air, water, and noise pollution. In this context, conservationists advocated setting aside so-called landscapes for recovery (*Erholungslandschaften*) for the majority of West Germans now living in urban areas.[51]

The idea to set aside scenic "peaceful oases" (*Oasen der Ruhe*) in nature for relaxation and recreation, though hardly new, was revived in 1956 by the wealthy Hamburg businessman and chairman of the *Verein Naturschutzpark* (VNP), Alfred Toepfer. According to Toepfer, West Germany, with only one large nature park in the Lüneburg Heath reserve, lagged far behind other densely populated nations such as Japan (seventeen parks) and Great Britain (ten parks) in providing the public with an important social amenity. Extensive media coverage popularized the plan to establish nature parks, each at least fifty thousand acres in size, as a way to address public health and, in Toepfer's initial conception of the program, to preserve nature and strengthen love of the *Heimat*.[52]

According to the initial promotional campaign led by the VNP and supported by the Federal Ministry of Agriculture, the preservation of nature was necessary for the health of the nation's labor force and the health of the country's economy. After spending time in natural surroundings, urban dwellers could return to their jobs, fully restored, ready to work.[53] Toepfer originally intended for nature parks to be established in some of West Germany's most popular scenic landscapes, such as the Eifel, the Alps, the Taunus Forest, and the Black Forest, that were reminiscent of the country's preindustrial past (and of Toepfer's own experiences in the *Wandervogel* movement). Setting aside a few aesthetically pleasing rural landscapes would, it was hoped, preserve them from development and, moreover, rekindle a love of *Heimat*. Implicit in his outdated and somewhat elitist vision was an assumption that preserving scenic landscapes representative of the country's regional *Heimaten* would strengthen ties to an imagined German *Heimat*,[54] a worthy goal because of the belief that urban dwellers had become alienated from nature. Preserving relatively undeveloped landscapes in a static state had nostalgic appeal because of the contrast these spaces would provide with the urban setting increasingly dirtied by soot, dust, noise, and noxious gases. Furthermore, establishing large parks near urban areas seemed to some to be an ideal way to accommodate economic growth while promoting public health and protecting nature.

Regional planners, who quickly seized upon the idea and integrated it into broader planning considerations, objected to such a backward-looking vision, however. Nature parks, they insisted, were not about preserving landscapes that recalled a bygone era from the inevitability of social and economic change or to provide people with a contrast to modern mass society. According to these experts, nature parks had to be planned with West Germany's future in mind. They did not have to be erected in areas that were particularly scenic or pristine (because West Germany had no pristine nature left). Rather, parks needed to be established in less economically developed areas of the Federal Republic, which had experienced population loss because of migration to cities and could no longer prosper on an agrarian-based local economy. Regional planners had confidence that rural landscapes could be made into attractive parks that would address the growing demand for recreation areas while also revitalizing the local economy by increasing tourism.[55] Moreover, nature parks, when carefully designed to harmoniously unify forests, farms, and villages, would serve as models for how to plan the use of the country's limited space and to balance competing and constantly fluctuating demands on the land.[56] Regional planners advanced the view that nature parks were essentially spaces that needed to be designed and ordered on a map, ultimately to bring economic prosperity to poorer areas.

Despite initial disagreement about the merits and primary purpose of the parks, the program found the support of the public and politicians irrespective of political party. By 1962, twenty-one parks covering roughly 2.5 million acres had been established across the country, primarily in Hesse, North Rhine-Westphalia, and Rhineland-Palatinate. In the mid-1970s, fifty-four nature parks extended over ten million acres, or approximately 16 percent of the total area of West Germany.[57]

Preservation had been the top priority for the initial promoters of the nature parks, but it was recreation that received emphasis during the first decade of the program. Thus, nature in the form of large parks was protected in a way that supported an affluent consumer society enjoying the fruits of economic prosperity. Outfitted with miles of trails, lookout towers, camping grounds, ski lifts, youth hostels, restaurants, and other facilities, all of the nature parks helped to satisfy growing consumer demand for recreation areas.[58] Not only in the Federal Republic, but also in other industrial societies, spending time in nature had come to be regarded by many as something to consume to enhance the quality of life. While nature parks helped to satisfy the growing demand in an affluent society for nonmaterial goods, they tolerated the negative aspects of prosperity rather than challenge them. The parks had been established to address the ills associated with urban, industrial society, but setting aside "peaceful oases" in rural areas where city people could escape for a day did little to confront those problems directly. In addition, a number of conservationists noted with frustration, the parks did pitifully little to protect nature.[59]

The program, however, marked a significant step in fundamentally altering how conservationists understood their work and what it meant to protect nature. In a concrete way, nature parks mirrored the urban industrial condition of the Federal Republic. For every metropolitan area, there was a nature park close by, linked by an ever-expanding network of highways. As cities stretched outward into the countryside, blurring the distinction between urban and rural, the work of protecting nature intersected more frequently with urban and regional planning. Conservationists agreed with regional planners in insisting that protecting nature, whether in the form of small reserves, scenic landscapes, or recreational parks, had to be pursued in conjunction with urban development.[60]

Closer cooperation between conservation and regional planning elevated the importance of protecting nature while simultaneously subordinating it to broader planning considerations. Until the late 1950s, state-sponsored conservation, with its estimated 500 honorary commissioners who aided conservation officials, had been able to do little more than adopt a defensive approach to protecting nature, often reacting to rather than preventing damage caused by development. The country's 750 nature reserves, 3,800 protected landscapes, 38,000 natural monuments, and 12 nature parks in 1960 attested to successes in traditional preservation. But the amount of land protected in these parks and reserves appeared insignificant when one considered that every year in West Germany an area estimated at 100 square miles was gobbled up by the expansion of housing, transportation, and industry.[61] Thus, state-sponsored conservation assumed a more active role in planning the use of land. Conservation agencies at the state and lower government levels participated in preparing plans that guided development or restored ecological order to landscapes, working hand-in-hand with regional planners who intended to prevent and correct disorderly development that was in part a consequence of liberal economic policies.[62]

The cause of protecting nature only indirectly received more attention when worsening pollution captured media headlines and became a focus of Willy Brandt's unsuccessful bid for chancellor in 1961.[63] That year, conservationists repeated their warnings that human beings had radically altered their surroundings to such an extent that these areas had become denatured and harmful to public health. As members of the German Horticulture Society announced in their Green Charter of Mainau in August 1961, "the basic foundations of our life have fallen into danger because vital elements of nature are being dirtied, poisoned and destroyed." Drafters of the charter maintained that "the worth of human beings is threatened where their natural environment (*Umwelt*) is damaged." Grounded in the Basic Law's protection of human dignity, liberty, and the right of inheritance, the Green Charter asserted that a "healthy living space" (*gesunder Lebensraum*) in city and country was a basic inviolable human right.[64] The Green Charter did not generate widespread support for protecting nature, but it did lead to the creation of the German Council for Care of the Land (*Deutscher Rat für Landespflege*). This body, comprised of academics, landscape architects, public officials, and prominent individuals, commissioned studies and advised the federal president and national and state ministries on a number of complex issues and projects, such as canalizing the Mosel, recultivating strip-mining areas, and managing solid waste. A less tangible consequence of the charter was the important legacy it left in asserting that a healthy space in which citizens could live fully and realize their potential was fundamental to improving the quality of life.

The Federal Republic was hardly alone in devoting more media and government attention to conservation and especially pollution issues between the late 1950s and early 1960s. Some scholars argue that this increased concern about nature, air, water, and the quality of life in cities at the end of the 1950s reflected a tendency in industrialized countries to shift attention to the negative aspects of development after a period of steady economic growth. This, they point out, had been the case not only in the late 1950s, but in the 1890s and 1920s as well. It is possible that conservationists' amplified fears expressed a desire not to halt economic growth, but to distribute the fruits of prosperity more evenly among the population. Only by conveying their message with a sense of urgency could they convince people to be more prudent in their treatment of nature and natural resources.[65]

In the West German context, it is curious that this urgency was expressed for a time with the term "living space" (*Lebensraum*). This concept, undeniably tainted because of its centrality in Adolf Hitler's plan for a greater, "purer" Germany became, fifteen years after the end of the war, a part of discourse about protecting nature. In searching for a term that would convey how the work of conservation had come to be an integral part of protecting public health and imposing greater order on the country's limited space, some turned to this concept, which means habitat. During the two previous decades, conservationists had explained that their work involved preserving and restoring the household or ecological health of landscapes and noted that "healthy" referred to land that was fertile, productive, free of pollution harmful to human health, and capable of healing people under stress.[66] These formulations stressed that tending nature was essential to human health and welfare, but emphasized non-human nature. This terminology failed to convey fears that human beings, in their increasingly unhealthy habitat, urgently needed to be protected.

The concept *Lebensraum* more effectively communicated an awareness of the reciprocal relationship between humans and their surroundings. People had changed their surroundings to the extent that they had become less natural, and thus perceptibly harmful to their health. Appeals to secure a healthy *Lebensraum* conveyed an understanding of the need to confront the cumulative effects of vast new problems, such as air and water pollution, excessive use of pesticides, the loss of plant and animal species and "green spaces" that threatened West Germans wherever they lived. As DNR President Hans Krieg explained to a deputy in the Bundestag in 1961, it was essential to address "all of those questions that affect our living space." The present organization of state-sponsored conservation, with its lack of funding and qualified official personnel would amount to little more than "pitiful piecework" (*klägliches Stückwerk*), he insisted, when faced with the task that would assume more importance in the coming years—the protection of living space.[67] Krieg proposed the establishment of a new *Lebensraum* ministry that would have departments responsible for water, air, the landscape (which, he explained, included social hygiene and climate, parks, reserves, and toxins in the landscape), protection of plants and animals, and control of pesticides. Krieg was calling, in short, for a ministry of the environment. Adenauer did not establish a ministry for protection of *Lebensraum*, but he did create a new Ministry for Health Affairs in 1961 that assumed responsibility for air, noise and water pollution, and public health.[68]

In the 1960s, conservation came to involve transforming the places where West Germans conducted their daily lives into more natural, habitable environs. As prominent conservationist Konrad Buchwald warned, unprecedented demands on the "landscape, as living space," and the stress "or even destruction of the natural bases of life—water, air, soil, and natural vegetation" had altered the urban environment, threatening human health.[69] He observed that inhabitants of densely populated cities worked unnatural hours at an unnatural pace under artificial light. Noise, foul air, polluted water, and surroundings more often cement than green, constituted the self-created, unnatural, technical environment of people in industrial society. Citing the federal government's regional planning report from 1963, Buchwald asserted that "soil, water, air, flora and fauna served as the foundations of the human environment." Since World War II, however, the human-created ersatz world of managed forests and farms, housing developments and industrial complexes, highways, airways, and railway lines had been layered more thickly over the natural world, rapidly replacing it. One of the most pressing social issues for advanced industrial countries, he asserted, involved bringing "order to the relationship between modern man and his environment."[70] Implicit in this challenge was the assumption that if humans had played a significant role in constructing this unhealthy environment, then they could, through better land-use planning and landscape design, restore a more healthy natural order to it as well.

Doing so required more effective regional and land-use planning, but also a clearer and more precise understanding of just how unhealthy the human environment was. In the 1960s, the work of conservation received attention from an expanding core of professionals—many of them outside of official conservation—who were trained in diverse fields of specialization but shared an understanding of ecology. As was the case on the international level, West German experts more frequently expressed their goals in abstract terms of assessing the productive capacity (*Leistungspotential*) of nature, or estimating the tolerance level (*Belastungspotential* or *Belastbarkeit*) of a landscape. Such discourse indicated an expectation that rational planning, guided by an ecological perspective, would provide the means to measure the stresses on nature, restore a landscape to ecological health, or provide a cost-benefit analysis of using natural resources to yield optimum results. The advantages of this technocratic approach were apparent, but so, too, were its shortcomings. At the request of the West German government, the Federal Institute for Conservation concluded a study in 1969 that inventoried the "Strain on the Landscape" from industrialized agriculture, construction, mining, pollution, and waste disposal. Though the report detailed how these problems compromised soil fertility, water purity, climate, and the stability of plant and animal communities, a lack of scientific data made it difficult to assess their cumulative effects.[71]

Influential international conferences, such as the 1968 Man and the Biosphere Conference in Paris sponsored by UNESCO, repeatedly called attention to the need for more effective national policies to protect ecosystems and address the social and cultural costs of environmental decline. Because environmental problems transcended national boundaries, delegates to the conference emphasized, it was important to confront them not only regionally and nationally, but on the international level as well.[72] Against this backdrop of heightened international concern about the biosphere, West German conservationists sought to strengthen efforts to protect nature through ecosystem research, land-use and regional planning, and a new federal guideline law for conservation. A minority proposed that the Federal Republic demonstrate its commitment to nature preservation also by establishing a national park, the country's first. With so many pressures contributing to a denatured environment, some insisted that the state had to assume greater responsibility for protecting nature to ensure that some parts of the country remained "natural."

The idea of establishing national parks had been discussed since the beginning of the twentieth century, but most West Germans thought that their country lacked the space to preserve large tracts of land where economic uses were restricted, if not ruled out entirely. In 1966, the plan resurfaced in the context of regional planning in the Bavarian Forest, an area with the highest rate of unemployment and the lowest income per capita in the Federal Republic. A general migration of people out of the area for more prosperous urban centers left the region in economic trouble. The extreme climate, dense forests, and location along the Iron Curtain contributed to its underdeveloped economy. After attempts to lure industry to the area had failed, regional planners and state government officials hoped to rescue the region from its economic troubles by developing the Bavarian Forest into a sought-out tourist destination.[73]

Deciding the form that this tourist attraction would take, however, generated fierce debate among groups engaged in conservation. Bavaria's forestry officials hoped to continue managing the state-owned land to ensure that the mixed forests remained economically productive as well as accessible to visitors seeking recreation in well-tended woods. Others, led by Alfred Toepfer, suggested erecting another nature park to add to the thirty-three already in existence in the late 1960s. In a nature park, year-round recreation would be balanced with forestry, farming, hunting, and the preservation of nature. A small contingent of conservationists led by the popular television personality and DNR President Bernhard Grzimek and an emerging leader in conservation, Hubert Weinzierl, envisioned a third, more radical course. Convinced that the country's nature reserves were far too small to protect ecosystems and that nature parks and landscape reserves emphasized recreation at the expense of preservation, they insisted that the country needed at least one reserve where nature was truly protected.

Grzimek pointed out that other nations of the world had national parks where stringent preservation of nature was carefully balanced with public recreation and scientific research, but not the Federal Republic. With no unaltered nature left to speak of in the late 1960s, West Germans of present and future generations were on the verge of losing an important part of their natural heritage. The "primeval landscape" in the Bavarian Forest, he insisted, offered the "last possibility" for establishing a national park that would satisfy the desire of West Germans to see wild animals and unspoiled nature.[74] According to Grzimek's initial plan for a national park, the carefully managed forest that had been shaped by centuries of human settlement would need to be returned to a supposedly more natural condition that resembled its state prior to extensive use. His plan called for recreating a landscape reminiscent of a bygone era, where the bison, lynx, wild boar, beaver, and chamois that had inhabited the forest in the early Middle Ages would once again roam the region. To support the reintroduction of wildlife, trees would need to be felled to create meadows for grazing. Once the park was returned to a "more natural" state, stringent preservation could be practiced (no forestry, hunting, or fishing).[75]

Grzimek, Weinzierl, Wolfgang Engelhardt, and other conservationists proposed the idea to Bavarian government officials in 1966. Three and a half years and many heated debates and expert opinions later, the Bavarian parliament called upon the state government to set aside thirty-three thousand acres of land in the Bavarian Forest for a national park. Any national park requires management to keep nature "natural," but after the Bavarian Forest was officially opened in 1970, transforming this landscape into a national park that conformed to international standards required years of extensive planning and management. Specialists prepared an ecological map of the region to aid in reconstructing the "original" distribution of trees, vegetation, and the wildlife the land had supported. Straightened streams were returned to what planners deemed to be a more natural course, and dams were built to flood areas and create wetlands. Bison, wolf, wild boar, otter and lynx were among the animals that made their new home in large enclosures on the outer zone of the park. Unlike in nature parks, however, in this national park almost a third of the area was under stringent protection and eventually allowed to evolve on its own to a large degree.[76]

Erecting this first national park in West Germany was not an overtly nationalistic undertaking. The Bavarian Forest was singled out for protection not because it was hallowed ground that symbolized a mythical national character, but because it was a unique, sparsely populated landscape situated in a region in economic trouble. Even the debate leading up to the park's establishment generated little interest or media coverage beyond the state level. Once opened, the park was, and still is, administered by the state government (as are the country's other national parks).

But the decision to erect the national park was significant. It indicated that the Federal Republic was affluent enough to afford the "loss" of a remote corner of the nation where good use of land meant little or no use for the sake of preserving nature and rare plant and animal species. Furthermore, creating a national park out of a carefully managed forest underscored the challenges of protecting nature in a country that had no unaltered nature left. The Bavarian Forest National Park was nature that initially had to be made "more natural" with extensive management to conform to the international definition of a national park. But as the debate over the forest revealed, there were conflicting ideas about nature and how it ought to be protected.

Establishing the national park enabled West Germany to protect nature and the economy locally in the Bavarian Forest, to support public recreation and preserve natural beauty in the nation, and to participate in the international effort to create a healthy, green environment. Erecting a national park along the border with Czechoslovakia provided a way not to defend West Germany's national boundaries, but to transcend them. If the Iron Curtain divided these two nations, the ecosystem of the Bohemian (Sumava) and Bavarian Forests, the largest continuous woodland in Central Europe, united them.

The national park was officially opened in 1970 as the "crowing point" of European Conservation Year (ECY) in the Federal Republic. Planned by the

Council of Europe beginning in 1963, European Conservation Year was intended to raise public awareness about human threats to nature and to promote international cooperation in managing the continent's natural resources. In West Germany, Chancellor Willy Brandt acted on his promise made earlier in his first policy statement before the Bundestag (October 1969) to devote more attention to conservation by appointing Grzimek to the new post of federal conservation commissioner.[77] But the environment, more so than protection of nature, received the most attention during ECY. It was the Social Democratic Party's partner in the coalition, the Free Democratic Party, that contributed most to the social construction of the environment, making it a tangible sphere of political activity. Hans-Dietrich Genscher (FDP), the new minister of the interior, sought to expand his area of competence by making protection of the environment (*Umweltschutz*) a legitimate issue of concern.[78] To the consternation of conservationists, however, the government's environmental program of 1970-1 did little to address "biological environmental protection" (*biologischer Umweltschutz*). Primary attention was devoted to technical measures aimed at reducing pollution rather than protecting nature and ecosystems in the environment.[79] This emphasis stemmed in part from Genscher's own conviction that "whoever develops the most modern environmental technologies will win the markets of the future."[80]

The concept "environment" was popularized in 1970 during European Conservation Year, particularly after the government announced its comprehensive program. Despite initial confusion about the meaning of the term in 1970,[81] "environment" quickly became popular in public discourse, in part because of its ability to form a variety of permutations, from environmental hygiene (*Umwelthygiene*) and environmental design (*Umweltgestaltung*) to environmental politics (*Umweltpolitik*) and environmental crisis (*Umweltkrise*). It seemed that the days were long gone when *Heimat* and national prosperity could rally the public around the cause of protecting nature. *Umwelt* communicated the reciprocal relationship between human beings and their surroundings, and in a more neutral way than the concept *Lebensraum*. With growing fear that people had altered their surroundings to such an extent that they would in turn affect humanity in ways that threatened their health and their very survival, it was important to underline this reciprocal relationship. In addition, *Umwelt* and *Umweltschutz* communicated not only the concern to safeguard one's local surroundings, it also underscored the international dimensions of the challenge to protect the planet. But some complained that the word "environment" was vague and devoid of a sense of definite place. *Umwelt* signified any of the many environments—biological, social, cultural, political, economic, recreational—that had become the "natural" world in which West Germans conducted their daily lives. One thing remained fixed: people were at the center of concern.

Debate over environmental policies and increased awareness about the imperiled state of the planet raised public awareness about the environment, and its defense generated a new form of political activism in the early 1970s, citizens' initiatives. Single-issue citizens' initiatives, 75 percent of which occurred after 1970, focused on a variety of concerns, from energy and transportation, to housing and the protection of rural areas.[82] In 1972, just after the United Nations Conference on the Human Environment in Stockholm, fifteen citizens' initiatives united to form the Federal Association of Citizens' Initiatives for Environmental Protection (*Bundesverband Bürgerinitiativen Umweltschutz*, BBU). By the end of 1975, BBU included 100 regional and local citizens' initiatives, claiming over 300,000 members. The emergence of these activists, who tended to be drawn from a younger generation of West Germans on the left of the political spectrum, initially gave traditional conservation organizations hope that they had finally attracted a broader base of support for their cause. But it quickly became apparent that citizens' initiatives preferred their own unique structure and organization and did not want to be absorbed by older groups. Citizens' initiatives indeed expanded the base of West Germans committed to environmental issues, but also contributed to more diverse approaches to nature and environmental protection. Citizens' initiatives had in common with traditional groups a desire to see that the state protected the right of citizens to a healthy environment, and the environment that they sought to protect and shape was usually their local environment, that which an older generation previously had called *Heimat*. When the state moved to decrease dependence on oil in 1973 by increasing reliance on nuclear power, citizens' initiatives focused their energies on the anti-nuclear campaign, working often outside of established political parties (despite being supported initially by the FDP-led ministry).[83] By the late 1970s, it was apparent to many that only an alternative political party committed to deep social change and a less exploitative living style could eliminate nuclear power and moreover, halt the destructive impact of modern mass society on people and nature. These frustrated citizens—some radical, others conservative—joined forces with the peace movement and thereby helped lay the ideological foundations of the Green Party.[84]

By the 1970s, protecting nature had been elevated to a higher level of significance than ever before, but simultaneously had become but a small part of protecting the imperiled human environment. With "the environment" an arena of political activity, conservation organizations and citizens' initiatives established spheres in which they could exert influence. The DNR, for example, hoped to become the dominant organization promoting *Umweltschutz*, but the organization's efforts were overshadowed to an extent by the more radical tactics of the BBU. By the mid-1970s, a variety of new groups vied for public support in fulfilling their visions of a healthy environment.[85]

With a limited amount of space and no unaltered nature to speak of, West German environmentalists, broadly defined, understood that it did little good to bemoan the loss of untouched nature. Rather citizens needed to make informed moral choices and rely on democratic processes to decide where and how to ensure that part of their environment retained varying degrees and forms of "naturalness." Sometimes those decisions would involve leaving nature alone to a large degree to return to a state that showed little evidence of human intervention, as was the case in parts of the Bavarian Forest National Park. The invention of the environment not only in West Germany but elsewhere in the 1970s indicated that those who wanted to protect nature saw themselves less and less as defenders of a "natural" world that existed apart from their own sphere of everyday activity. Rather, they were the primary architects of their local, national and international environment, responsible for daunting task of determining how and where to cultivate it in varying degrees of "naturalness."

Notes

1. Neil Evernden, *The Social Creation of Nature* (Baltimore, 1992), xii.

2. Fairfield Osborne, *Our Plundered Planet* (New York, 1948); William Vogt, *The Road to Survival* (New York, 1948); Adolph Metternich, *Die Wüste droht. Die gefährdete Nahrungsgrundlage menschlichen Gesellschaft* (Bremen, 1947).

3. Gert Kragh, "Gesunde Landschaft bedingt die Zukunft des Volkes," a report submitted to the Oberpräsident of Lower Saxony, December 13, 1945, Bundesarchiv, Koblenz, Bundesamt für Naturschutz (hereafter BAK B245/153). This report also is published in Walter Mrass, "Zu einigen Organisations- und Zielmodellen für Naturschutz und Landschaftspflege zwischen 1935 und 1945," *Natur und Landschaft* (hereafter *N & L*) 56, no. 7/8 (1981): 271-3. On the concept "inner colonization," see Woodruff Smith, *Politics and the Sciences of Culture in Germany, 1840-1920* (Oxford, 1991), 227.

4. Gert Kragh, "Gesunde Landschaft bedingt die Zukunft des Volkes."

5. For an overview, see Alfred Barthelmess, *Landschaft, Lebensraum des Menschens. Probleme von Landschaftsschutz und Landschaftspflege* (Munich and Freiburg, 1988); and Norbert Fischer, "Der neue Blick auf die Landschaft: Die Geschichte der Landschaft im Schnittpunkt von Sozial-, Geistes-, und Umweltgeschichte," *Archiv für Sozialgeschichte* 36 (1996): 434-42.

6. William Rollins, *A Greener Vision of Home: Cultural Politics and Environmental Reform in the German Heimatschutz Movement, 1904-1918* (Ann Arbor, 1997); Andreas Knaut, *Zürück zur Natur! Die Wurzeln der Ökologiebewegung* (Greven, 1993), 386-91.

7. Gert Gröning and Joachim Wolschke-Bulmahn, *Die Liebe zur Landschaft* vol. 1, *Natur in Bewegung. Zur Bedeutung natur-und freiraumorientierter Bewegungen der ersten Hälfte der 20. Jahrhunderts für Entwicklung der Freiraumplanung* (Munich, 1986); Gröning and Wolschke-Bulmahn, *Die Liebe zur Landschaft*.vol. 3, *Der Drang nach Osten. Zur Entwicklung der Landespflege im Nationalsozialismus in den 'eingegliederten Ostgebieten' während des Zweiten Weltkriegs* (Munich, 1987); Klaus Fehn,"'Lebensgemeinschaft von Volk und Raum': Zur nationalsozialistischen Raum- und Landschaftsplanung in den eroberten Ostgebieten," in Joachim Radkau and Frank Uekötter, eds., *Naturschutz und Nationalsozialismus* (Frankfurt, 2003), 207-24.

8. Konrad Buchwald, *Die Zukunft des Menschen in der industriellen Gesellschaft und die Landschaft* (Braunschweig, 1965), 43. See also Gerhard Helmut Schwabe, "Zur Landschaftsökologie," *N & L* 36, no. 5 (1961): 65-67; Wolfgang Engelhardt, *Umweltschutz. Gefährdung und Schutz der natürlichen Umwelt des Menschen* (Munich, 1973), 41-42.

9. Hans Klose [Director of the then Central Agency for Conservation] to Karl Duve [State Commissioner for Conservation, Hamburg], May 27, 1947, BAK B245/137. Struck from the preamble were phrases stating that care of natural monuments "only partially could be effective

because the essential political and ideological conditions were lacking. Only the transformation of the German *Volk* created conditions for effective *Naturschutz.*" In addition, Paragraph 18 of the RNG was omitted which had empowered the state to dispossess property owners without compensation if it was necessary for establishing Reich nature reserves. This paragraph also had provided for an agency in charge of confiscating land and resettlement. Finally, Paragraph 12 of the 31 October 1935 ordinance for enforcing the law was deleted. It had empowered Hermann Goering, in conjunction with other ministers, to confiscate land for the preservation of nature.

10. K.-G. Kolodziejcok, "Die Entwicklung des Naturschutzrechts in der Bundesrepublik Deutschland," *N & L* 50, no. 1 (1975): 4. Under West Germany's Basic Law the states assumed primary jurisdiction over conservation; the federal government had the power only to enact guideline laws.

11. *Reichsgesetzblatt* (1935) I. no. 68, 821-26. For an overview of the passage of the RNG, see Michael Wettengel, "Staat und Naturschutz 1906-1945. Zur Geschichte der Staatlichen Stelle für Naturdenkmalpflege in Preußen und der Reichsstelle für Naturschutz," *Historische Zeitschrift* 257 (1993): 382-7. On the RNG in the context of other conservation and environmental legislation passed under the Nazis, see Edeltraud Klueting, "Die gesetzlichen Regelungen der nationalsozialistischen Reichsregierung für den Tierschutz," in *Naturschutz und Nationalsozialismus*, 77-105. On conservationists' failed attempt to address shortcomings in the RNG during the Third Reich, see Walter Mrass, "Zu einem fast dreißig Jahre alten Änderungsentwurf des RNG," *N & L* 46, no. 1 (1971): 15-16.

12. For example, the Ministry of Culture served as the highest conservation office in Lower Saxony, Baden-Württemberg, Rhineland-Palatinate and Saarland. The Ministry of Agriculture had responsibility for conservation in Hessen and Schleswig-Holstein, while the Ministry of the Interior assumed this task in Bavaria. In North Rhine-Westphalia the Ministry of Housing and Public Works oversaw conservation. See Walter Mrass, *Die Organisation des staatlichen Naturschutzes und der Landschaftspflege* (Stuttgart, 1970), tables 10-17.

13. These conservation agencies had evolved out of volunteer committees first organized in the early 1900s in Prussia, Bavaria, Saxony, and other states to advise and pressure officials. See Raymond Dominick, *The Environmental Movement in Germany: Prophets and Pioneers, 1871-1971* (Bloomington, 1992), 49-53; Knaut, *Zuruck zur Natur!*, 386-91.

14. Mrass, *Organisation des staatlichen Naturschutzes*, 40-1, and tables 10-17, 23; Klose, "Über die Lage der Landes- und Bezirksstellen," *Verhandlungen Deutscher Beauftragter für Naturschutz und Landschaftspflege* (hereafter *Verhandlungen*) (1948): 5; Karl Koch, "Hemmungen und Misserfolge unserer Arbeit," *Verhandlungen* (1948): 11; "Haushaltsmittel für Naturschutz und Landschaftspflege," *Verhandlungen* (1956): 120-21, 126-8.

15. The institute had a history dating back to 1906 in Prussia, when it was founded as the State Agency for the Care of Natural Monuments (Staatliche Stelle für Naturdenkmalpflege). It was elevated to the status of Reich Agency for Conservation (Reichsstelle für Naturschutz) in 1935. After World War II the institute became the Federal Institute for Conservation (Bundesanstalt für Naturschutz und Landschaftspflege, BANL). After being merged with the institute for plant cartography (Vegetationskartierung) from 1962 until 1976, the institute was renamed the Federal Research Institute for Conservation and Landscape Ecology (Bundesforschungsanstalt für Naturschutz und Landschaftsökologie). It is currently the Federal Office for Conservation (Bundesamt für Naturschutz).

16. See Klose, "Über Arbeitsziele und Arbeitsmethode der Reichsstelle für Naturschutz," September 19, 1945, BAK B245/238; and Klose to Administration of Nutrition, Agriculture and Forestry [Federal Ministry of Agriculture], June 27, 1950, BAK B245/247; Kragh, "Gesunde Landschaft bedingt die Zukunft des Volkes."

17. Erich Hornsmann, *Innere Kolonisation oder 'Man Made Desert'* (Stuttgart, 1948), 9-10.

18. Wilhelm Lienenkämper, "Gedanken zur Tätigkeit der Naturschutzbeauftragten," *Verhandlungen* (1949): 35. See also Carl Duve, "Landschaftspflege in der Stadtlandschaft," *Verhand-*

lungen (1948):18-20; Arne Andersen, *Der Traum vom guten Leben. Alltags- und Konsumgeschichte vom Wirtschaftswunder bis heute* (Frankfurt/Main, 1997), 127-8.

19. United States Office of Military Government for Germany (hereafter OMGUS), *A Year of Potsdam: The German Economy Since the Surrender*, prepared by the Director of the Economic Division, Brigadier General William H. Draper, Jr. (Washington, D.C., 1946), 69-70; OMGUS, *Special Report of the Military Governor, The German Forest Resources Survey*, 1 October 1948, no. 40, 7; Hinrich Wilhelm Kopf, typed copy of "Bericht des Sonderausschusses 'Erhaltung des deutschen Waldes,' Detmold, April 26, 1946," BAK B245/230.

20. Institut für Besatzungsfragen, *Einwirkung der Besatzungsmächte auf die Westdeutsche Wirtschaft* (Tübingen, 1949), 105-6; Frank Roy Willis, *The French in Germany, 1945-1949* (Stanford, 1962), 138-9; Freda Utley, *The High Cost of Vengeance* (Chicago, 1949), 278-79; "Aus der Geschichte der SDW," *Unser Wald* 39, no. 5 (1987): 157.

21. OMGUS, *Special Report of the Military Governor, The German Forest Resources Survey*, 1 October 1948, no. 40, provides a comprehensive overview of the nature and extent of forest resources in all four zones, with emphasis on the American zone. For an overview of the different approaches to timber harvesting in the western zones of occupation, see Institut für Besatzungsfragen, *Einwirkung der Besatzungsmächte auf die Westdeutsche Wirtschaft*, 99-109. For a concise discussion of criticisms of timber harvesting in the French zone see Willis, *The French in Germany*, 138-9; Carolyn Eisenberg, *Drawing the Line. The American Decision to Divide Germany, 1944-49* (Cambridge, 1996), 234.

22. These complicated issues are discussed in a number of places. See for example Hinrich Wilhelm Kopf, typed copy of "Bericht des Sonderausschusses 'Erhaltung des deutschen Waldes,' Detmold, April 26, 1946," BAK B245/230; Typed text of a lecture, "Holz und Forstwirtschaftsfragen," delivered at the Vollversammlung der Industrie und Handelskammer Braunschweig in Lebenstedt, September 12, 1947 in BAK B245/230.

23. On German attitudes toward the occupying powers and their tendency to blame the Allies for many of the difficulties of the immediate postwar years see Barbara Marshall, "German Attitudes to British Military Government 1945-1947," *Journal of Contemporary History* 15 (1980): 655-84; Josef Fochepoth, "German Reaction to Defeat and Occupation," in Robert G. Moeller, ed., *West Germany under Construction: Politics, Society, and Culture in the Adenauer Era* (Ann Arbor, MI, 1997), 73-89.

24. Baumgartner delivered these comments during the June 1947 minister-presidents' conference in Munich, which convened heads of state governments of all four zones to discuss essential economic questions. See Document 32A, "Ministerpräsidentenkonferenz München," June 6-7, 1947, item 10b, "Diskussion über die Referate zur deutschen Wirtschaftsnot, Wald- und Holzfrage," in *Akten zur Vorgeschichte der Bundesrepublik Deutschland 1945-1949*, ed. Bundesarchiv and Institut für Zeitgeschichte, vol. 2, *Januar 1947 – Juni 1947*, ed. Wolfram Weiner (Munich, 1982), 545-7.

25. Ibid., 547. See also "Protokoll der Gründungs-Versammlung und ersten Arbeitstagung der 'Schutzgemeinschaft Deutscher Wald', Bad Honnef," December 5, 1947, BAK B245/230.

26. Kurt Borchers, *Der Wald als deutsches Volksgut* (Lüneburg, 1948), 67-73. See also Schutzgemeinschaft Deutscher Wald, *Uns ruft der Wald. Ein Buch deutscher Dichter und Waldfreunde* (Rheinhausen, 1949).

27. "Protokoll der Gründungs-Versammlung und ersten Arbeitstagung der 'Schutzgemeinschaft Deutscher Wald'"; pamphlet entitled, "Der deutsche Wald ist in Gefahr!" n.d. [December 1947?], BAK B245/230. On efforts to engage the youth, see Karl Korfsmeier, "Der Wald im Schulunterricht," *Grünes Blatt* (March 1949): 2; Sigmond, "Jugend und Walderneuerung," *Grünes Blatt* (November 1948): 9; idem, "Unser Wald ruft die Jugend," 1-2; summary of Lehr's comments at annual meeting of the main SDW organization in May 1949, *Grünes Blatt* (July/August 1949): 2. On the involvement of the youth in reforestation see *Forst- und Holzwirtschaftlicher Informationsbrief der SDW* (27 May 1948): 2, in BAK B245/230; "So will es

die Jugend," *Grünes Blatt* (October 1949): 13. See also Wilhelm Lienenkämper, *Grüne Welt zu treuen Händen. Naturschutz und Landschaftspflege im Industriezeitalter* (Stuttgart, 1963), 157.

28. For an overview of how the oak acquired significance in Germany as a symbol of freedom during the French Revolution and of national unity later in the nineteenth century, see Annemarie Hürlimann, "Die Eiche, heiliger Baum deutscher Nation" in *Waldungen. Die Deutschen und Ihr Wald,* ed. Akademie der Künste (Berlin, 1987), 62-9.

29. At the time Robert Lehr, a member of the Christian Democratic Union, was serving as federal minister of the interior, an office he held from 1950-3.

30. Excerpts from Lehr's speech appear in "Westdeutschland feiert den 'Tag des Baumes,'" *Nachrichtenblatt für Naturschutz* 23, no. 5/6 (May/June 1952): 13.

31. Excerpts from Adenauer's comments appear in "Treubekenntnis zum deutschen Wald," *Unser Wald,* no. 3 (1953), clipping in BAK B245/231.

32. Celia Applegate, *A Nation of Provincials: The German Idea of Heimat* (Berkeley, 1990), 229, 242-3.

33. The poll was conducted at the request of the Schutzgemeinschaft Deutsches Wild. See "Zur Erhaltung des Wildbestandes. Ergebnisse einer Bevölkerungs-Umfrage," May 1955, table II, BAK B245/242.

34. Typed copy of newspaper article in *Harburger Anzeiger und Nachrichten,* June 25, 1956, in BAK B245/83.

35. Konrad H. Jarausch, Hinrich C. Seeba, and David Conradt, "The Presence of the Past. Culture, Opinion, and Identity in Germany," in Konrad H. Jarausch, ed., *After Unity. Reconfiguring German Identities* (Providence, 1997), 40-1.

36. The Protective Association of the German Forest (*Schutzgemeinschaft Deutscher Wald*), the Protective Association for German Wildlife (*Schutzgemeinschaft Deutsches Wild*), the Alliance for Protection of Germany's Waters (*Vereinigung Deutscher Gewässerschutz*), and the German Working Group for Fighting Noise (*Deutscher Arbeitsring für Lärmbekämpfung*) all emerged in the late 1940s or early 1950s.

37. By 1964, the IPA had 300 members. Dominick, *Environmental Movement in Germany,* 191, 194, 200; Günter Küppers, Peter Lundgreen and Peter Weingart, *Umweltforschung—die gesteuerte Wissenschaft? Eine empirische Studie zum Verhältnis von Wissenschaftentwicklung und Wissenschaftspolitik* (Frankfurt/Main, 1978), 102-3.

38. Sandra Chaney, "Visions and Revisions of Nature. From the Protection of Nature to the Invention of the Environment in the Federal Republic of Germany, 1945-1975," Ph.D. diss., University of North Carolina-Chapel Hill, 1996, 123-35; Otto Kraus, "Vom Primat der Landschaft (1949),"in *Zerstörung der Natur. Unser Schicksal von morgen? Der Naturschutz in dem Streit der Interessen,* ed. Kraus (Nuremberg, 1966), 10-13.

39. On the debate surrounding the Wutach, see Chaney, "Visions and Revisions of Nature," 183-228. On the Mosel, see Chaney, "Water for Wine and Scenery, Coal and European Unity: Canalization of the Mosel River, 1950-1964," in Susan C. Anderson and Bruce H. Tabb, eds., *Water, Culture, and Politics in Germany and the American West* (New York, 2000), 227-52.

40. Chaney, "Water for Wine and Scenery, Coal and European Unity," 227-52.

41. Friedrich Schnoor to Federal Chancellery, April 26, 1956; Franc Griller to Federal Chancellery, April 22, 1956, both in Politisches Archiv, Auswärtiges Amt, Bonn, Abteilung 2 (Politische Abteilung), Referat 217, Aktenzeichen 372-08 E, Band 3 (hereafter cited as PA/AA/Abt. 2/Ref.217/Az. 372-08 E/Bd. 3).

42. See Liese-Lott Mergert to Federal Chancellery, May 4, 1956; Friedrich Schnoor to Federal Chancellery April 26, 1956; Dr. jur. Ernst Waag to Federal Chancellery, March 26, 1956; Walter Schumacher to Adenauer, April 18, 1956; Friedrich Enkemann to Federal Chancellery, April 4, 1956; Ilse Friedhoff to Federal Chancellery, April 21, 1956; Kurt Schaefer (for Bundesführung der FKK Jugend, Bund der Lichtscharen) to Adenauer, April 8, 1956; Westfälischer Naturschutztag telegram to Federal Chancellery, May 5-6, 1956, all in PA/AA/Abt. 2/Ref.217/Az. 372-08 E/Bd. 3.

43. Resolution of the Landesfischereiverband Rheinland-Rheinhessen e.V. (Hillesheim, Chairman), n.d. [late June? 1956], PA/AA/Abt. 2/Ref.217/Az. 372-08 E/Bd. 3.

44. Klaus-Georg Wey, *Umweltpolitik in Deutschland: kurze Geschichte des Umweltschutzes in Deutschland seit 1900* (Opladen, 1982), 173-81.

45. Among the many letters and postcards that spurned "sacrificing" the Mosel to accommodate France's economic interests, see Ilse Friedhoff to Federal Chancellery, April 21, 1956; Anita Lefeldt to Federal Chancellery, April 7, 1956; Martin Höppner to [not specified], May 5, 1956; Jürgen [Tomm?] and 21 other youth to Federal Chancellery, April 1956; Henry Brockhahne to [not specified], May 14, 1956, all in PA/AA/Abt. 2/Ref.217/Az. 372-08 E/Bd. 3

46. Liese-Lott Mergert to Federal Chancellery, May 4, 1956, PA/AA/Abt. 2/Ref. 217/Az. 372-08 E/Bd. 2.

47. Herbert Frank to Federal Chancellery, May 8, 1956. PA/AA/Abt. 2/Ref. 217/Az. 372-08 E/Bd. 3.

48. Floristisch-Soziologische Arbeitsgemeinschaft (Dr. Erich Oberdorfer) to Foreign Office, April 6, 1956; Arbeitsgemeinschaft Rheinisch-Westfälischer Lepidopterologen, e.V., Celle (Dr. Max Cretschmar) to Federal Chancellery, April 26, 1956; Arbeitsgemeinschaft der Westdeutschen Vogelschutzwarten (W. Hahn) to Foreign Office, April 12, 1956; Anita Lefeldt to Federal Chancellery, April 7, 1956.

49. Joachim Bodamer, *Gesundheit und technische Welt* (Stuttgart, 1960); Konrad Buchwald, "Gesundes Land—Gesundes Volk. Eine Besinnung zum Gesundheits- und Erholungsproblem," *N & L* 32, no. 6 (1957): 94-8.

50. This shift in understanding was also apparent in other industrialized nations. On the United States, see Samuel Hays, *Beauty, Health and Permanence: Environmental Politics in the United States, 1955-1985* (Cambridge, 1987).

51. For a more general discussion of consumer behavior and uses of increased leisure time in West Germany, see Axel Schild, " 'Mach mal Pause!' Freie Zeit, Freizeitverhalt und Freizeit Diskurse in der westdeutschen Wiederaufbau-Gesellschaft der 1950er Jahre," *Archiv für Sozialgeschichte* 33 (1993): 357-406; Schild, "Freizeit, Konsum und Häuslichkeit in der 'Wiederaufbau'-Gesellschaft. Zur Modernisierung von Lebensstilen in der Bundesrepublik Deutschland in den 1950er Jahren," in Hannes Siegrist, ed., *Europäische Konzumgeschichte: zur Gesellschafts- und Kulturgeschichte des Konsums (18. bis 20. Jahrhundert)* (Frankfurt am Main, 1997), 327-48; Andersen, *Der Traum vom guten Leben.*

52. Alfred Toepfer, "Naturschutzparke—eine Forderung unserer Zeit," *Naturschutzparke* (Autumn 1957): 172, 174.

53. See the film "Naturschutzparke—Kraftquellen unseres Volkes," produced by Eugen Schuhmacher [1957?] in Verein Naturschutzpark Archive, Niederhaverbeck, Lüneburg Heath (hereafter VNP Archive).

54. This analysis relies on Alon Confino, "The Nation as a Local Metaphor: *Heimat,* National Memory and the German Empire, 1871-1918," *History and Memory* 5, no. 1 (Spring/Summer, 1993): 62-3, 64.

55. Erich Dittrich to Toepfer, September 10, 1959, Verband Deutsche Naturparke Archive, Niederhaverbeck, Lüneburg Heath, binder # 45, labeled "Bundesbehörde und Anstalten" (herafter cited as VDN Archive, #45, "Bundesbehörde und Anstalten").

56. Dittrich, "Der Ordnungsgedanke der Landschaft und die Wirklichkeit," *Verhandlungen* (1959): 128; Gerhard Isbary, "Naturparke als Vorbildslandschaften," in *Das Naturpark-Programm und seine Probleme,* Schriftenreihe des Vereins Naturschutzpark e.V., ed. Verein Naturschutzpark e.V. (Stuttgart and Hamburg, privately published, n.d. [1962?]): 30.

57. Hans-Dietmar Koeppel, "20 Jahre Naturparkprogramm—Finanzierung und aktueller Entwicklungsstand," *N & L* 51, no. 5 (1976): 130.

58. Ulrich Nickel and Walter Mrass, "Zum Entwicklungsstand der Naturparke in der BRD," *N & L* 48, no. 6 (June 1973): 163-72. A thorough analysis of the nature park program is pro-

vided by Udo Hanstein, *Entwicklung, Stand und Möglichkeiten des Naturparkprograms in der Bundesrepublik Deutschland—ein Beitrag zur Raumordnungspolitik* (Stuttgart, 1972).

59. Bernhard Grzimek to Toepfer, April 17, 1967, Deutscher Naturschutzring Archive, binder labeled "Nationalpark Bayerischer Wald, 1966-67" (hereafter DNR Archive, "Nationalpark Bayerischer Wald, 1966-67"); Wey, *Umweltpolitik in Deutschland,* 200.

60. Dittrich, "Der Ordnungsgedanke der Landschaft und die Wirklichkeit," *Verhandlungen* (1959): 127-34.

61. Heinrich Lohmeyer, "Unser Lebensraum ist in Gefahr!" *N & L* 36, no. 3 (1961): 34, 36.

62. Dittrich, "Vom Schutz der Natur zur Ordnung der Landschaft," *N & L* 34, no. 5 (1959): 65-6; "Ordnung der Landschaft—Ordnung des Raumes. Bericht über den Deutschen Naturschutztag Bayreuth, vom 22. bis 27. Juni 1959," *N & L* 34, no. 8 (1959): 113-7.

63. Lienenkämper, *Grüne Welt zu treuen Händen,* 82; Dominick, *Environmental Movement in Germany,* 183-7; Wey, *Umweltpolitik in Deutschland,* 187.

64. Lienenkämper, *Grüne Welt zu treuen Händen,* 82. See also "Grüne Charta von der Mainau," *N & L* 36, no. 8 (1961): 151.

65. Dominick, *Environmental Movement in Germany,* 183-7; John McCormick, *Reclaiming Paradise: The Global Environmental Movement* (Bloomington, IN, 1989), 49.

66. Buchwald, *Die Zukunft des Menschen in der industriellen Gesellschaft und die Landschaft,* 43.

67. Hans Krieg to an unidentified Bundestag deputy, October 24, 1961, abbreviated version sent to Gert Kragh, BAK B245/235.

68. Dominick, *Environmental Movement in Germany,* 200.

69. Buchwald, "Der Mensch in der Industriegesellschaft und die Landschaft," *N & L* 36, no. 12 (December 15, 1961): 212.

70. Buchwald, *Die Zukunft des Menschen in der industriellen Gesellschaft und die Landschaft,* 7.

71. A summary of the report is provided by Olschowy, "Zur Belastung der Biosphäre," *N & L* 44, no. 1 (1969): 3-6.

72. United Nations Educational, Scientific and Cultural Organizations, *Use and Conservation of the Biosphere. Proceedings of the Intergovernmental Conference of Experts on the scientific basis for Rational Use and Conservation of the Resources of the Biosphere, Paris, 4-13 September 1968* (Paris, 1970). The official title of the conference was the "Intergovernmental Conference of Experts on the Scientific Basis for Rational Use and Conservation of the Resources of the Biosphere." See also Rainer Piest, "Die wissenschaftlichen Grundlagen für eine rationale Nutzung und Erhaltung des Potentials der Biosphäre," *N & L* 44, no. 4 (1969): 94; McCormick, *Reclaiming Paradise,* 88-90. The conference brought together approximately 350 delegates representing sixty-three countries and an estimated thirty international organizations such as the World Health Organization, the Food and Agriculture Organization, and the International Union for the Conservation of Nature. West Germany sent eleven delegates, including Konrad Buchwald and BAVNL director, Gerhard Olschowy.

73. Georg Kluczka, " 'Raumordnung'—Regional Planning and Spatial Development," in Peter Schöller, Willi Walter Puls, and Hanns J. Buchholz, eds., *Federal Republic of Germany: Spatial Development and Problems,* (Paderborn, 1980), 11-17, esp. 13-15; Michael Haug, "Entstehungsgeschichte des Nationalparks Bayerischer Wald," in Bayerisches Staatsministerium für Ernährung, Landwirtschaft und Forsten, ed., *Eine Landschaft wird Nationalpark,* Schriftenreihe des Bayerischen Staatsministeriums für Ernährung, Landwirtschaft und Forsten, vol. 11 (Grafenau, 1983), 40.

74. Franz Handlos, "Grzimek: letzte Möglichkeit für Nationalpark," *Münchner Merkur,* July 28, 1966, 8, clipping in Schutzgemeinschaft Deutscher Wald Archive, Bavarian Chapter, Munich, file labeled "Nationalpark Bayerischer Wald, vol. I, Zeitungsartikel" (hereafter cited as SDW Archive/NPBW/I/Zeitungsartikel).

75. Grzimek to Bavarian Ministry of Agriculture, Forestry Department, August 5, 1966, DNR Archive, "Nationalpark Bayerischer Wald, 1966-67."

76. Michael Haug, "Wozu ein Nationalpark in Deutschland?" *N & L* 47, no. 5 (1972): 131; Erik Spemann, "Nationalpark: Es geht nicht nur um wilde Tiere," *Münchner Merkur*, October 7, 1970, clipping in SDW Archive/NPBW/Zeitungsartikel.

77. Dominick, *Environmental Movement in Germany*, 197; "Nichts zu tun," *Der Spiegel*, June 29, 1970, p. 31.

78. Horst Bieber, "Langsam stirbt der Umweltschutz. Von deutscher Naturromantik zur politischen Macht—doch der alte Schwung ist hin," *Die Zeit*, October 20, 1978, 8; Küppers, Lundgreen, and Weingart, *Umweltforschung—die gesteuerte Wissenschaft?* 128-9; Wey, *Umweltpolitik in Deutschland*, 201; Franz-Josef Brüggemeier, *Tschernobyl, 26 April 1986. Die ökologische Herausforderung* (Munich, 1998), 208-9.

79. Hermann Josef Bauer and Gerhard Olschowy, "Zum Umweltprogramm der Bundesregierung," *Jahrbuch für Naturschutz und Landschaftspflege* (1972): 98; Werner Hoffmann, "Naturschutz in der Entscheidung—ausder Sicht des Fachmanns," *Jahrbuch für Naturschutz und Landschaftspflege* (1972): 34.

80. Hans-Dietrich Genscher, *Erinnerungen* (Berlin, 1995), 126.

81. Wolfgang Erz, "Europäisches Naturschutzjahr 1970—und was wurde erreicht?" *N & L* 45, no. 12 (1970): 410.

82. Udo Kempf, "Bürgerinitiativen—der empirische Befund," in Bernd Guggenberger and Udo Kempf, eds., *Bürgerinitiativen und repräsentatives System*, 2d rev. ed. (Opladen, 1984), 297. Forty percent of citizens' initiatives addressed energy concerns (nuclear power); 33 percent focused on transportation; and 32 percent on protection of the countryside. See Bernd Guggenberger, "Umweltpolitik und Ökologiebewegung," in Wolfgang Benz ed., *Die Geschichte der BRD*, vol. 3, *Economics* (Frankfurt/Main, 1989), 398.

83. Joachim Raschke, *Soziale Bewegungen. Ein historisch-systematischer Grundriss* (Frankfurt/Main, 1985), 205, 213; Werner Hülsberg, *The German Greens: A Social and Political Profile*, trans. Gus Fagan (New York, 1988), 57.

84. See Dieter Rucht, *Von Wyhl nach Gorleben: Bürger gegen Atomprogramm und nukleare Entsorgung* (Munich, 1980), 80; Karl-Werner Brand, Detlef Büsser, and Dieter Rucht, eds., *Aufbruch in eine andere Gesellschaft. Neue soziale Bewegungen in der Bundesrepublik* (Frankfurt/Main, 1983), 89-102.

85. Chaney, "Visions and Revisions of Nature," 419-32.

Chapter 6

WALDSTERBEN
The Construction and Deconstruction of an
Environmental Problem

Franz-Josef Brüggemeier

Waldsterben, "forest death," became a key political issue in Germany during the early 1980s. A whole generation of school children grew up with the fear that German trees and forests would soon be dead and gone. Newspapers, radio, and television programs fuelled the fire. It was impossible to ignore the subject. And it was this very issue that galvanized the environmental movement in Germany and brought it to the forefront of mainstream politics. *Waldsterben* has remained on the political and environmental agenda ever since. It is seen as a critical problem without a solution in sight.

A few years ago, however, findings were published that contradict the established view. They question the belief that widespread *Waldsterben* was and indeed is still taking place, but the findings have not been readily accepted. We now have two diametrically opposed viewpoints. My paper will ask how these views came about, what premises they are based upon—how they were constructed—and it will analyze the current situation.

My argument will be developed in four stages. First, I will summarize the debate that took place in the 1980s: scientists' expectations, people's fears, the German media's reaction. Second, I will look at debates on dying trees and forests in Germany over the past two hundred years. In the third part of my paper, I will return to the current debate and present the latest scientific findings into the state of German and European forests—with some surprising results. Finally, I will draw some conclusions on the construction and deconstruction of environmental and, more generally, historical debates.

Notes for this section begin on page 130.

* * *

The debate on dying forests began quite abruptly. The German weekly magazine *Der Spiegel* ran a three part series in November of 1981 on the poisoning of German forests by acid rain. There had been one or two reports on this subject within the recent past, but those had dealt primarily with specific regions and were not noticed by the public at large. The articles in *Der Spiegel*, however, described dying forests as a problem that affected not only some regions but all of Germany, Europe, and indeed the entire world—with catastrophic consequences for all.[1]

Der Spiegel, buttressed by quotes from scientists, claimed that a time bomb was ticking in the forests. Conifers were dying on a large scale. They were only the harbingers of a "worldwide, environmental catastrophe of an unimaginable scale."[2] Foresters were alarmed because they found that conifers were aging too quickly. They reckoned that more than 50 percent of the forests were endangered. According to them, the prime reason for all this was "an increase in air pollution, particularly in sulfur dioxide (SO_2) from oil-based central heating, exhaust pipes, and, above all, from emissions generated by power plants, iron foundries, and refineries."[3]

Bernd Ulrich, a biologist from Göttingen University, claimed that large forests would be "dead within the next five years. They cannot be saved." Additionally, there would be damage to buildings and river pollution, affecting the health of children, the aged, and the infirm. Furthermore, these dangers were equally great for Eastern and Western Europe, Scandinavia, Japan, the United States, and Canada. Damage would be worldwide and uncontrollable, because acid rain from Japan could fall on America; emissions from the U.S. could reach Canada, and the European states were polluting each other, depending on the prevailing winds.[4]

Pollution was already widely debated in the 1980s, but the discussion of *Waldsterben* was the first time that the general public became aware of how complex environmental pollution was, how far it could reach, and how it extended beyond national borders. The debate on the environment had reached a new level. The articles in *Der Spiegel* sparked a new, fierce public controversy. In the following months and years, *Waldsterben* appeared almost daily in German newspapers and magazines. Radio and television followed suit. Numerous books appeared on the subject, parliamentary commissions were set up, and other countries were so impressed by this debate that the word *Waldsterben* was introduced into their languages. In 1984, *Stern*, another influential German weekly magazine, reported that two out of seven million acres of German forests were either dying or already dead. The mountains of the Harz forest were slowly turning into a lunar landscape; foresters reported a dramatic increase in the number of dying trees. Besides conifers, beech, oak, elm, and cherry trees had also been affected. The illness caused by pollution was eating its way through the countryside like a cancer. According to *Stern*, experts had declared that there would be no conifer forests left in Germany by 1990 and that the beech forests would disappear shortly thereafter. *Stern* cited a report commissioned by the Federal Ministry of the Interior that went even further: by the year 2002, there would be no dying forests in Germany—not because of an unexpected remedy or recovery, but simply because "hardly any forests would be left."[5] And that would only mark the beginning of further problems. For once the forests had disappeared, floods and avalanches would follow; villages and roads in the Alps and other mountainous regions would have to be abandoned.

From that point on, reports on *Waldsterben* were issued every year. They confirmed existing fears, and the 1984 report came to the conclusion that more than 50 percent of the West German forests were already damaged.[6] These figures were seen as somewhat optimistic, the report continued, since ailing or dying trees had already been cut and were not reflected in these statistics. Only the pathologically ignorant could question the extent of the damage as experts made grim forecasts. The head of the state forestry office in Baden-Württemberg, for example, claimed, "We cannot escape the harsh reality that we are facing the beginning of a catastrophe in our forests brought about by pollution if we do not succeed in reducing pollution drastically and immediately." BUND, the leading environmental pressure group, spoke of an ecological Hiroshima, and the Greens coined the motto: "First, the trees will die and then people!"[7]

The debate had started without warning. In 1975, the Ministry of the Interior still thought of sulfur dioxide as a local problem of no special importance. Three years later, in 1978, the Office for Environmental Affairs in the state of North Rhine-Westphalia pointed out that outside the heavily industrialized Ruhr Valley damaged trees were found only in a few isolated areas, usually near industrial plants. There were no calls for a drastic reduction of sulfuric emissions. Even the owners of forests did not call for such measures, nor did they show much interest in the problem of "traveling pollution." Instead, they looked for ways to secure compensation should damage occur. It was not until 1979, after studies in Scandinavia had shown that air pollution and sulfuric emissions in particular could travel over huge distances, that they asked for more information on the problem of sulfuric emissions.[8]

* * *

The public was taken by surprise when the debate on *Waldsterben* broke out in the 1980s. To be sure, similar debates had taken place 200 years earlier, but nobody remembered them at the end of the twentieth century. Furthermore, the environmental controversies of the late eighteenth century had not been about industrial pollution—industrialization did not take off in Germany until the 1840s—but about the reduction of timber stocks. It was believed that the practice of felling trees was denuding German forests and would lead to a dramatic shortage of wood. And wood was by far the most important resource at that time. It was used for building houses, ships, and carts; many objects and tools for daily use were also made of wood. Wood was irreplaceable in heating homes and other buildings, smelting iron, producing glass, et cetera. Coal was not widely used, and no other alternative resource was in sight. A scarcity of wood would therefore have caused great hardship. Consequently, the complaints about the situation were highly dramatic. In 1785, for example, one of the numerous publications on this topic maintained that there was scarcely any wood left, that prices were sky-rocketing, and that people could not afford to heat their homes.[9] In 1798, another author pointed out that the complaints about the shortage of wood could be heard everywhere. Trade and industry would soon have to cease, he continued, and the situation was getting desperate for the populace.[10] Propelled by fear, people called on the government to do something.[11]

The problem had arisen because a large population increase over the previous decade had led to increased wood consumption. Consequently, this resource was becoming more and more expensive in many areas, and nobody could see an end to this situation. Governments felt obliged to intervene. Among other measures, they issued decrees on reducing wood use. In some places, wood-gathering, an ancient right of the poor, was forbidden. New laws regulating the use of the forests were issued, and in general the powers of the bureaucrats in charge of the forests were increased. In addition to these measures, there were widespread attempts to use wood and forests more efficiently. Many inventors boasted that their newly constructed ovens would use much less wood; others sought to improve chimneys and smelting techniques. In addition, modern scientific knowledge and methods in forest management, which had only just been developed, were applied. New forests were planted on a wide scale; conifers were preferred on account of their rapid growth. All of this seems to have been successful because complaints more or less stopped during the early decades of the nineteenth century, long before coal made any significant contribution.

Several decades later, around 1850, another debate concerning trees and forests took place.[12] This time, it was a more "modern" debate, that is, it dealt with the effects of industrial pollution. The debate started in Freiberg, a small town near Dresden in the eastern part of Germany. Freiberg was home to an iron foundry that had been smelting iron for centuries but had recently increased its production significantly. Iron ore contains a high level of sulfur, which escapes when heated and can cause serious damage. This had happened all along, but now the quantities and therefore the damaging effects were much larger. The population of the surrounding villages therefore complained to the government, which sent Julius Adolph Stöckhardt, a scientist from a nearby university, to investigate the situation. His report left no doubts. "The effect on the vegetation was devastating," he wrote. "One could even say that pollution has had a disastrous effect." Fruit and grass were in poor condition, and there were stretches of land "from which all vegetation had disappeared." To Stöckardt, it was evident that the smoke from the foundry was responsible for these conditions and that above all sulfuric acid had had a "very negative influence on the vegetation."[13]

This report started a long debate that continued until the turn of the century. During this period, systematic experiments were carried out on animals and plants; technical solutions were developed; chimney stacks built higher and higher; and even farming techniques changed as part of the effort to reduce the ill effects of pollution. In 1860, for example, a new chimney came into use that was over 180 feet high. The results, however, offered little consolation. Even at that height, the chimney did not eliminate pollution. Rather, noxious substances were carried into neighboring forests, and the damage affected a greater area than before. Over time, there was a "noticeable increase in ailing and dying pine trees."[14] There was an additional problem: the strong updraft needed to carry the sulfuric acid to greater heights also lifted other noxious substances as well. The suction was so strong that large amounts of metallic oxides, particularly arsenic acids, were also carried into the air. But because these were heavy metals, they fell on the surrounding areas and poisoned animals. High chimneys improved the situation close to the foundry but at the same time increased the radius of damage. A report from 1861 stated: "The smoke was spread over a wider area, and damaged places it had previously not been able to reach."[15]

In the 1880s, an even higher chimney stack was built. It was well over 400 feet high and remained the tallest in Europe until 1928. This chimney was more efficient in thinning out pollution, but even it could not render it harmless. Damage now occurred six miles away, and it became clear that poisonous waste did not just disappear. Experience elsewhere was similar. Bernard Borggreve, a contemporary scientist, summed up the findings in the conclusion that "once something is in this world it cannot simply be made to go away again."[16]

People had in fact been aware of this all along, and tall chimneys had not been built by mistake or simply on account of some naive faith in the advance of technology. On the contrary, high chimneys were chosen since other alternatives were even less effective. In Freiberg, many experiments were carried out to contain the noxious substances, among them special chambers to hold back the soot; newly constructed furnaces; the installation of pipes that fit as tightly as possible; the addition of chalk and other materials to cause chemical reactions that would rid the smoke of poisonous gases. Similar attempts were made in other places, since these problems were not restricted to Freiberg. There was even an international exchange of information on these experiments. By and large, the results remained disappointing, not so much for lack of trying, but more because of insufficient knowledge of physics and chemistry, rudimentary technical know-how, the want of materials that could stand up to the enormous heat and pressure, and similar factors.

Some of the experiments carried out in Freiberg showed how complex the problems were. Julius Adolph Stöckhardt, for example, tried to determine the damage caused by different levels of sulfuric acid. In his experiments he exposed plants to varying concentrations of this substance and was able to thin it down to a ratio of 1:1,000,000. Even then, damage still occurred, albeit after a longer period of time and with less severity.[17] And it is exactly such results which were and still are a major problem in dealing with emissions. Emissions rarely show their effect immediately or in a way that establishes clear connections between cause and effect. Normally, they produce long range effects, causing only slight symptoms at first, not even very specific symptoms at that, but symptoms which could equally be caused by different factors. Damage to plants, for example, could be the result of emissions. It could, however, also be caused by drought, lack of fertilizers, by fungi, or a variety of other factors, producing similar reactions. Even with sophisticated, modern equipment and advanced knowledge, it is—almost as a matter of course—still difficult to prove beyond any doubt that specific damage has been caused by a specific pollutant.

A Freiberg experiment with animals confirmed the complexity of the problem. Cows became ill in the area surrounding the foundry. People wondered whether this was due to the influence of the fumes and, if so, which particles were responsible. Since hardly anything was known about this problem, the commission set up experiments with animals, probably the first in Germany, to determine the effects of pollution. Viewed from a modern perspective, this experiment was anything but convincing. The scientists in Freiberg had very little money and could only afford to buy one cow. However, after a couple of weeks they abandoned the experiment, knowing full well that they could not expect serious results using just one animal. They therefore bought two oxen. One was given polluted fodder, the other non-polluted. The first ox lost weight as had been expected. When the experiment was repeated, it produced a similar result. The evidence therefore seemed convincing, but a closer look left much to be desired as one of the scientists involved pointed out.

It was not enough to prove that a substance was poisonous. Given in high quantities almost anything, including beer, he declared, is poisonous. The real task involved was to define critical levels. This, of course, required more than one or two oxen. Furthermore, once the animals were slaughtered and examined the scientists did not know what to look for. Their understanding of the animal body and the processes caused by the polluted fodder was too limited. To increase their knowledge, they wanted to buy twelve sheep and feed each sheep a different quantity of polluted fodder. Unfortunately, their funding ran out, and the experiment had to be abandoned.[18]

Though severely limited, these experiments still produced interesting results and formed the basis for scientific research into air pollution in Germany. But, as is often the case, a gulf existed between scientific progress and everyday problems. The scientists had not been successful in identifying clear criteria to differentiate between damage caused by pollution and other factors. Furthermore, they had established that pollution in high concentrations produced ill effects, but they could not determine what the safe limits were—a problem that is still difficult to solve even today.

The scientists, therefore, faced enormous difficulties. But it must be stressed that almost 150 years ago they had already accumulated a great deal of knowledge on the subject of air pollution. The dangerous effects of sulfuric acid in particular had been scientifically proven, and many attempts were made to do something about them. Huge technical problems were involved, but the costs in bringing about solutions had to be considered as well. Without going into this matter in more detail, it can be stated that, more often than not, it was cost that prevented the adoption of effective measures.[19] As a consequence, pollution increased, particularly in heavy industrialized areas like the Ruhr Valley. It was there that an interesting conflict took place in the early 1920s.

In 1923, the French marched into the Ruhr Valley. The occupation of the area was met by passive resistance by the population. Industry came to a halt, the supply of coal ran out, and trees were chopped down to make fuel. While the population had to suffer hardships, nature profited from the occupation. Passive resistance started in spring and was abandoned in autumn. This meant that industrial production, and with it pollution, stopped during the period of growth for most vegetation. One witness gave the following description of what happened:

> When the production of coal, coke, and steel came to a halt, the population quickly noticed a clear improvement in the air in the Ruhr basin, so much so, that there was no longer any difference between this region and a non-industrial area. The effect of this change on vegetation was amazing. The results could best be observed on root vegetables. Their leaves remained green until well into the autumn, whilst their leaves had usually withered in early summer.... Potatoes, which are known to be particularly sensitive to smoke, grew at an unprecedented rate.... Bare patches started to turn green again. In previous years only two harvests had been possible. Now there were three unusually large harvests.... The produce was so plentiful that it met not only home demand, but could also be sold on the market. This had never happened before.... Fruits were clean and not covered by a thin layer of soot, dust, or tar.[20]

Even the tree rings were thicker in 1923 than in the previous or following years.

Passive resistance ended in the autumn of 1923. Industrial production resumed, much to the relief of the population that had suffered enormously. For the vast majority, there was no doubt what conclusions to draw from this experience. Everybody had seen how damaging industrial pollution was to vegetation. Again committees were set up to investigate the problem and to draw up proposals to remedy the problem. But the population also realized that smoking chimneys and industrial pollution were necessary for their livelihood, and that was where their priorities lay. Of all the proposals submitted by the committees, only one was accepted: to look for and plant trees which could put up with industrial pollution.[21]

* * *

These examples—more could be found—show that several waves of debates on air pollution and dying trees or *Waldsterben* waxed and waned in Germany over the last two centuries. In between it seemed, that many of the scientific results were almost forgotten, so that the renewed debate of the 1980s could take most people by surprise. But the basic knowledge gained earlier had only been forgotten, not lost. It could be recovered quickly and brought up to date by new research. The experts, therefore, could base their warnings on a large foundation of findings, which had been gathered over decades.

This long, scientific tradition was rediscovered by the media, and, of course, by environmental historians. The study of the past only increased their skepticism towards government policy. Obviously, the consequences of air pollution, especially of sulfuric acids, had been known for over a hundred years, yet very little had been done, the emissions had been ignored. As late as the 1970s, the policy of building higher and higher chimney stacks was still the primary way of dealing with air pollution. To be sure, this had brought relief to heavily polluted areas like the Ruhr basin, since the emissions were transported out of the region and carried higher and further away. But—as in Freiberg more than a century ago—the polluting substances did not disappear; they fell on different regions and have affected the forests there. The policy of the high chimney had obviously failed. A new start had to be made.

This new beginning came surprisingly quickly. Gerd Baum, the Federal Minister of the Interior, was under so much pressure that he decided to take a "great leap forward" in environmental politics. In doing so, he also hoped to breathe new life into the crisis-ridden governing coalition of the Social Democrats and Free Democrats. Baum arranged for a special cabinet meeting to be called on September 1, 1982. Just one year after the debate had started, the cabinet agreed on strict limits for sulfur dioxide.[22] This decision was in part prompted by the sudden success of the Green Party, which had done amazingly well at the polls since its founding in 1980, not least as a result of the fears caused by the debate on *Waldsterben*. The government was therefore trying to give itself a new profile in environmental politics in order to attract support. Despite these measures, the coalition soon fell apart and was replaced in October 1982 by a new coalition of Christian Democrats (CDU/CSU) and Free Democrats. As a matter of principle, the new government wanted to reduce the role of the state and improve the situation for industry by reducing taxes and regulations. Business was particularly hostile to the new laws on reducing pollution since their implementation would be expensive. But the new government had to respond to the enormous public interest in *Waldsterben* as well as the Greens' election results. It therefore upheld the environmental laws and set even stricter limits for power plants, with the result that five years later, by 1988, almost all coal-fired generating plants possessed highly effective filters that held back more than 90 percent of the sulfuric acid.[23]

Additionally, great sums of money were made available for scientific research into the causes of *Waldsterben* and ways to end it. By the early 1990s, more than $100 million had been spent on research alone. The government also felt obliged to commission yearly reports on the state of the forests, which are still being issued today. But despite all these efforts, the problem has persisted. The latest reports claim that widespread damage still exists, so obviously there has hardly been any progress.

Waldsterben seems to be the perfect example of the inability of politicians to react to environmental problems and to listen to the warnings of scientists. The danger has not disappeared. Every year the same ritual takes place: the government publishes a new report and announces a slight improvement of the situation; the environmentalists complain about the continuing untenable situation and demand that more be done. They are supported by the owners of forests, who continue to hope for more compensation; the media feel obliged to report all this, while the public loses interest. It knows the story by heart and is bored with it. There is, however, a completely different and extremely interesting story to be told instead, though it is hardly ever told. It is a surprising story—if Heinrich Spiecker and his group of researchers are right.

Spiecker teaches at the Institute of Forest Growth (*Institut für Waldwachstum*) at the University of Freiburg in southern Germany. In recent years, he has led a group of international researchers from twelve different countries in examining the state of Europe's forests from 1900 until the present. Their findings were published in 1996, and they are astounding. Trees in Europe, even in Germany, are growing faster than ever before.[24] There can be no talk of forests dying. On the contrary, between 1950 and 1990 forest acreage in Europe increased by 43 percent, with Germany recording one of the largest increases. As the liberal *Frankfurter Rundschau* put it, "There's never been so much wood around."[25] It is only in a few places, especially impacted by pollution or exposed to bad weather, that trees have suffered and their growth has been affected.

The researchers were surprised by their own findings. It had been known that certain kinds of trees grew well in particular areas. But that had seemed to be an exception to the general state of affairs. Now it was discovered that this increase in growth was taking place all over Europe, in all sorts of places and involving almost all types of trees. The contrast to the thesis of *Waldsterben* could not have been greater.

Spiecker's group examined the height and width of the trees. This method is time consuming, but the results are very reliable. The methods which had prevailed until then are more debatable. They basically depended on an analysis of the tree-surface, i.e. the leaves or needles. The trees are then grouped into different categories according to their appearance, the number of their leaves or needles and their density. This method has the advantage of being easy to apply, especially when it comes to large areas. It is not necessary to cut trees and measure them, as the Spiecker group had to do. It is enough to inspect them closely.

This visual approach, however, has two main problems. For one, it is based upon appearance and the eye of the observer, so there is plenty of room for subjective judgment. Individual foresters come up with different ratings. Moreover, the question still remains what conclusions should be drawn from the state of the leaves or needles. Spiecker and others emphasize that their loss has to be interpreted very carefully. It is not at all clear to what extent this is the symptom of a damaged tree. For example, losing leaves could be a way for trees to protect themselves against drought. Furthermore, they continue to grow, even when their tops are almost bare. To use a rough comparison: the fact that a person loses or gains weight is not a clear indication of his/her health. Also, as critics of the *Waldsterben* thesis point out, it is natural that trees—like humans—sometimes fall ill. The fact, therefore, that we find damaged trees should not necessarily lead to alarmist predictions. And finally, if we find damaged trees, we have to look very carefully into possible causes. Ironically, an important factor seems to be the fear dating back to the eighteenth century that forests would disappear because of an over-consumption of wood. This, as pointed out, led to the large-scale planting of new forests. To get results quickly and to combat the fear that there would not be enough wood, many foresters preferred fast-growing conifers and relied heavily on monocultures. Both make for very vulnerable forests, and both may be a major reason for the damages that occurred in recent years.[26]

The contrast between the two schools of thought could not be greater. There is the claim, on the one hand, that the forests and their trees are growing more quickly than at any time in recent decades, but, on the other, there is still widespread fear that the forests are seriously damaged. It may be too early to decide which of the two claims is correct, but there seems to be little doubt that the thesis of widespread *Waldsterben* is difficult to uphold.

It is amazing that in all the media reports on the phenomenon of *Waldsterben* the new findings have hardly ever been mentioned. To be sure, there were a few articles and reports when the findings were first published. But one had to look very carefully to notice them. The interest they produced can in no way be compared to what went on in the early 1980s. More astonishingly, even the official reports on *Waldsterben* commissioned by the government look at the problem in the established ways and arrive, more or less, at the same conclusions as before. And that does not only apply to Germany. The reports commissioned by the European Union have also painted a picture of widespread damage to trees.[27]

This is difficult to explain. While there is no doubt that forests are still affected by emissions and much needs to be done about pollution, it is rather strange that in a public debate that has been and remains as intense as the one on *Waldsterben* conflicting findings are not being noticed, let alone taken into account. The debate remains very one-sided. In fact, one could argue that a proper debate has yet to take place, that for a great variety of reasons the controversy has been confined to a few experts. A few of these reasons should be mentioned.

It is obviously difficult to accept news that completely contradicts widely accepted knowledge and assumptions. The findings of Spiecker and his group do not just add a few unexpected results to commonly held views: they refute them completely. It seems to be almost impossible to integrate such findings into established knowledge. Rather, they tend to be seen as a product of someone's imagination that does not have to be taken seriously. This obviously also applies to journalists, even though Spiecker's arguments would make a fascinating story. It would allow them to shatter widely held views as a myth—which journalists normally enjoy doing. But so far this has not happened.

On another level, there seems to be fear that playing down the problem of *Waldsterben* would lead to complacency and thereby harm the environmental debate. It would, therefore, be better not to give too much weight to the new findings even if they are correct. In this context, an institutional explanation has to be considered as well. By now, there are a great number of institutions, scientists, lawyers, and pressure groups working on the problem of *Waldsterben*. Many of them started up in the 1980s and still identify strongly with the arguments developed at that time.

The debate on *Waldsterben* is an interesting example of how historical knowledge is being constructed. The different arguments described in this paper are based upon different methods of investigation, which themselves are constructed—as is the whole idea of *Waldsterben*. The notion of trees being sick, damaged, or dying is not self-evident. Trees, obviously, cannot tell us whether they are sick or dying. We have to do the diagnosing ourselves. *Waldsterben* in itself does not exist independently of researchers and their methods. For some, a tree that is losing its needles is sick; for others, it is protecting itself against drought; and a third group argues that this proves nothing at all. Of course, trees can be sick or dying. But to state such a fact, we have to construct a definition and establish clear criteria. The majority of the media in Germany still uphold the thesis of *Waldsterben*, while within the scientific community there is a growing consensus that refutes this idea.

In this context, environmental history is an interesting case in point. It obviously works with terms, concepts, and narratives that are constructed. At the same time, however, it deals with nature that exists not only as a construct, but that also has a reality of its own. Environmental history, therefore, not only serves as a corrective against excessive constructions but also makes us more aware of and careful about the concepts we use. It is nothing new that our definitions and interpretations of history depend on constructions and are influenced by special interest groups, specific ways of seeing a problem, institutional pressures, et cetera. A careful interpretation of primary sources, therefore, plays an important role in historical research, but too often we are not as critical when it comes to scientific statements or "facts."

Let us return to the debate on the shortage of wood at the end of the eighteenth century. A critical rereading of the sources has shown that this fear was grossly exaggerated. To be sure, there was an increasing demand for wood following the rise in population. This often led to price increases and occasionally to shortages of wood. A general shortage, however, did not occur. Rather, this claim arose from the motives of different interest groups. The owners of forests wanted to exploit the situation by stressing the scarcity of wood; above all, they were interested in raising prices and abolishing the traditional right of the poor to gather wood. The foresters as a newly established professional group stressed the coming crisis to increase their own powers and promote a newly developed, so-called scientific management of forests. Furthermore, the groups that traditionally had the right to harvest large quantities of wood seized the argument to hold back their competitors. Today, these arguments and interests are apparent, but they were not as apparent to contemporaries.

It seems that a similar story can be told about *Waldsterben* in the late twentieth century. Surely, in some places trees have suffered, their growth has been slowed and pollution played an important part. But on the whole, there is growing evidence that the damage neither was as widespread nor as serious as the *Waldsterben* thesis alleged. We might find, therefore, that our outlook of the 1980s and 1990s was perhaps too grim, and that *Waldsterben* was not so much an empirical phenomenon but rather a social and cultural construction.

Notes

1. "Säureregen: 'Da liegt was in der Luft,'" *Der Spiegel* 35, no. 47 (Nov. 16, 1981): 96-110; no. 48 (Nov. 23, 1981): 188-200; no. 49 (Nov. 30, 1981): 174-90.

2. *Der Spiegel* 35, no. 47 (Nov. 16, 1981): 96.

3. Ibid., 99.

4. Ibid., 101.

5. *Stern,* March 24, 1983, and July 5, 1984.

6. Bundesministerium für Ernährung, Landwirtschaft und Foresten, ed., *Waldschäden in der Bundesrepublik. Stand August/September 1984* (Münster-Hiltrup, 1985), 26.

7. *Die Zeit,* October 19, 1984, 17ff.; *Der Spiegel* 37 (February 14, 1983): 72.

8. Arbeitskreis Chemische Industrie Köln, Katalyse-Umweltgruppe Köln e.V., ed., *Das Waldsterben: Ursachen, Folgen, Gegenmaßnahmen* (Köln, 1984); Erwin Nießlein and Uwe Arndt, *Was wir über das Waldsterben wissen* (Köln, 1985).

9. "Abhandlung von der Holzersparung," *Lippstädter Bürgerblatt* 2 (1785): 1.

10. C.P. Laurop, *Freimüthige Gedanken über den Holzmangel* (Altena, 1798), V-VI.

11. Joachim Radkau, "Zur angeblichen Energiekrise des 18. Jahrhunderts: Revisionistische Betrachtungen über die 'Holznot,' *Vierteljahreshefte für Sozial- und Wirtschaftsgeschichte* 73 (1986): 1-37; Rolf-Jürgen Gleitsmann, "Rohstoffmangel und Lösungsstrategien: Das Problem vorindustrieller Holzknappheit," *Technologie und Politik* 16 (1980): 104-54.

12. For a detailed analysis of the conflict see Arne Andersen, *Historische Technikfolgenabschätzung am Beispiel des Metallhüttenwesens und der Chemieindustrie, 1850-1933* (Stuttgart, 1996), 45-225; Franz-Josef Brüggemeier, *Das unendliche Meer der Lüfte. Luftverschmutzung, Industrialisierung und Risikodebatten im 19. Jahrhundert* (Essen, 1996), 152-98.

13. Staatsarchiv Dresden Min. Inn. 16164, Bl. 29-61R, 02.03.1850; the report was published as Julius Adolph Stöckhardt, "Ueber die Einwirkung des Rauchs der Silberhütten auf die benachbarte Vegetation u.s.f.," *Polytechnisches Centralblatt* 16 (1850): 257-78.

14. Julius Adolph Stöckhardt, "Untersuchungen über die schädliche Einwirkung des Hütten- und Steinkohlerauches auf das Wachstum der Pflanzen, insbesondere der Fichte und Tanne," *Tharandter forstliches Jahrbuch* 21 (1871): 226.

15. Moritz Freytag, "Wissenschaftliches Gutachten über den Einfluß des Hüttenrauches bei den fiscalischen Hüttenwerken zu Freiberg auf die Vegetation der benachbarten Grundstücke und ganz besonders auf die Gesundheit der Hausthiere, namentlich des Rindvieh's" *Jahrbuch f. d. Berg- und Hüttenmann* (1873): 17; Staatsarchiv Dresden, MdI 16164, report by Reuning, July 7,1861, Bl. 402-4R, Bl. 404, and October 29, 1861, Bl. 425.

16. Bernard Borggreve, *Waldschäden im Oberschlesischen Industriegebiet* (Frankfurt/M., 1895), 32.

17. Andersen, *Historische Technikfolgenabschätzung,* 131-48; Brüggemeier, *Meer der Lüfte,* 177-82.

18. Freytag, "Wissenschaftliches Gutachten," 37-41; Gotthelf Carl Haubner, "Die durch Hüttenrauch veranlassten Krankheiten des Rindviehes im Hüttenrauchbezirke der Freiberger Hütten," *Archiv für wissenschaftliche und practische Thierkunde* 4 (1878): 97-136, 241-60; Andersen, *Historische Technikfolgenabschätzung,* 145-48; Brüggemeier, *Meer der Lüfte,* 177-79.

19. There is a rich literature on this topic in German. In addition to Andersen, *Historische Technikfolgenabschätzung,* and Brüggemeier, *Meer der Lüfte,* see Ulrike Gilhaus, *Schmerzenskinder der Industrie. Umweltverschmutzung, Umweltpolitik und sozialer Protest im Industriezeitalter in Westfalen 1845-1914* (Paderborn, 1995); Ralf Henneking, *Chemische Industrie und Umwelt* (Stuttgart, 1994); and the review article by Marc Cioc, Björn-Ola Linnér and Matthew Osborn, "Environmental Writing in Northern Europe," *Environmental History* 5 (2000): 397-407.

20. Heinz Bergerhoff, *Untersuchungen über die Berg- und Rauchschädenfrage mit besonderer Berücksichtigung des Ruhrbezirks* (Godesberg/Bonn 1928), 71-8.

21. Franz-Josef Brüggemeier and Thomas Rommelspacher, *Blauer Himmel über der Ruhr. Geschichte der Umwelt im Ruhrgebiet 1840-1990* (Essen, 1992), 50-4; Franz-Josef Brüggemeier, "A Nature fit for Industry. The Environmental History of the Ruhr Basin, 1840 – 1990," *Environmental History Review* 18 (1994): 35-54.

22. Wolfgang D. Müller, *Geschichte der Kernenergie in der Bundesrepublik Deutschland,* vol.1: *Anfänge und Weichenstellungen* (Stuttgart, 1990), 139, 308.

23. Hans-Peter Vierhaus, *Umweltbewusstsein von oben. Zum Verfassungsgebot demokratischer Willensbildung* (Berlin, 1994); Edda Müller, *Innenwelt der Umweltpolitik. Sozial-liberale Umweltpolitik – (Ohn)Macht durch Organisation,* 2nd ed. (Opladen, 1995); Franz-Josef Brüggemeier, *Tschernobyl – die ökologische Herausforderung,* (Munich, 1998), 222-50.

24. Heinrich Spiecker et al. eds., *Growth Trends in European Forests. Studies from 12 Countries.* (Berlin, 1996); see also Wolfgang Zierhofer, *Umweltforschung und Öffentlichkeit: Das Waldsterben und die kommunikativen Leistungen von Wissenschaft und Massenmedien* (Opladen, 1998).

25. *Frankfurter Rundschau,* November 24, 1996.

26. Hansjürg Küster, *Geschichte des Waldes. Von der Urzeit bis zur Gegenwart* (München, 1998).

27. See, e.g., United Nations, Economic Commission for Europe, ed., *Forest Conditions in Europe* (Geneva and Brussels, 2000).

INDEX